PRIEST LAKE MUSEUM PRESENTS

P I O N E E R
VOICES
of Priest Lake

Edited by
Kris Runberg Smith

KEOKEE
BOOKS

Sandpoint, Idaho

Cover photo by Leland Howard

Published by Keokee Co. Publishing and Priest Lake Museum

Keokee Co. Publishing, Inc.
P.O. Box 722
Sandpoint, Idaho 83864
(208) 263-3573
www.keokeebooks.com

People, places and dates were gleaned from oral histories and information on donated photographs.

First printing 2007
Printed in the United States of America

Publisher's Cataloging-in-Publication Data
Pioneer voices of Priest Lake / edited by Kris Runberg Smith
        Includes bibliographical references.
        Includes index.
        p.   cm.
        1. Priest Lake (Idaho)–history–personal narratives. 2. Frontier and pioneer life–Priest Lake (Idaho). 3. Priest Lake (Idaho)–history, local.
I. Title. II. Edited by Kris Runberg Smith.
979.69–dc21 2007
ISBN 978-1-879628-31-1

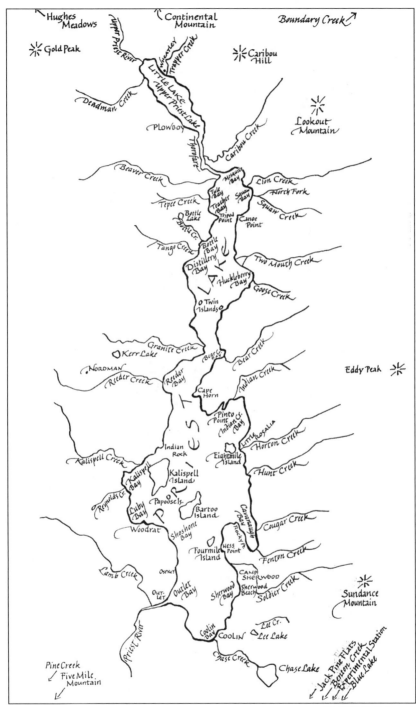

Map by Marita McDonough

Contents

ACKNOWLEDGMENTS

This project began when Charlotte and Hank Jones donated transcripts of Leonard Paul oral interviews to the Priest Lake Museum. It took form as Pam Martin and Jeanne Tomlin worked with Ann Ferguson from the Bonner County Historical Society (BCHS) on a Bonner County Centennial project. Shortly thereafter, it became reality when President JoAnn Becker and the Priest Lake Museum Association board of directors approved the project and pursued funding opportunities.

Pam Martin, Scott Hill and Marita McDonough served as photo editors for the book. They also contributed to research efforts, along with Ann Ferguson and Vern Eskridge of the BCHS, Kay Coykendall, Hank and Charlotte Jones, Marcella Cooper, and Mary Toutonghi. Regina Manser and Catherine Simpson were proofreaders for the manuscript. Jeanne Tomlin coordinated manuscript development, serving as copy editor. Special thanks to all for their enthusiastic support.

The Priest Lake Museum appreciates the generous contributions of the following individuals and organizations that made the publication of "Pioneer Voices of Priest Lake" possible. Because of their donations, proceeds from this book will support future museum efforts.

Priest Lake People Helping People, Inc.
Kaniksu Lions
JoAnn and Dave Becker
Marcella and James Cooper
Cindy and T.W. Dick
Gary and Joyce Fry
Teresa Myrwang Holum
       In Memory of Nancy Lou Myrwang
Charlotte and Henry Jones
David and Meridith Manlowe
Regina Manser
Scott and Nicole McKay
Entree Gallery
       Pam and Jim Martin
Dee and Mary Ann McGonigle
Joyce and Galen Miller
Myrwang Family
Brian Runberg and Katie Gjording
John S. Young

PREFACE

When Leonard Paul's granddaughter Charlotte Jones and her husband, Hank, retired back to Priest Lake in 1987, they discovered an 8 mm tape made by her mother years earlier. Marjorie (Paul) Roberts had captured her father's memoirs on tape. She preserved the words of a Priest Lake pioneer who not only witnessed years of change from his store's front porch but often played a role in shaping the lake's history as well. The transcript of the tape provided the inception for this book project and also lends a framework for each chapter. We were able to enhance Leonard Paul's recollections with the addition of the next generation of lake voices captured by the Priest Lake Museum through an oral history project begun in 1983. Together with a few additional primary sources, this book offers glimpses of Priest Lake before World War II through the words of those who actually experienced it.

Editing this book has brought me full circle with the Priest Lake Museum. As a graduate student in 1983, I created an oral history and photograph collection program for the museum through an Idaho Humanities Council grant. Many of the photographs in this volume were acquired during that initial project. I never imagined I would be editing those interviews more than 20 years later. It is sobering to consider that the voices we captured then are no longer with us. On one hand, there are so many questions I wish I could go back and ask. On the other hand, we are indeed fortunate to have preserved what we did. As in 1983, I continue to be impressed by the support, energy and commitment of the Priest Lake Museum volunteers.

When I was a child, our Coolin Bay cabin provided one of the stops for Leonard Paul's happy hour circuit. The fun began when he arrived in his beret with his cigar and bulldog. I don't

recall specific stories he and my grandmother, Vivienne Beardmore McAlexander, shared, but even at a young age I knew
that something magical was happening. After all these years, I
am honored to edit the oral histories of Leonard Paul and others who lived Priest Lake's early history.

This book has truly been a family venture. My mother,
Jeanne McAlexander Tomlin, served as copy editor and cheer-
leader; my brother, Brian Runberg, provided monetary support;
my husband, Dr. Jeff Smith, offered historical context; and my
daughter, Lucy Smith, endured as I spent time editing. My
contributions to this book are a memorial to my grandparents.
My grandfather, "Mac" McAlexander, encouraged my efforts to
organize the original oral history project and believed in the
importance of community. My grandmother, Vivienne Beardmore McAlexander, instilled a deep respect for our Priest Lake
heritage and introduced me through her memories to the men
and women who lived it.

Kris Runberg Smith
Editor

NOTES ON EDITING

Oral histories provide a wonderful window into the Priest Lake's past. They are especially important since more traditional documentation of the region is regrettably scarce. However, like all sources, these histories come with their own set of considerations. For this volume, I tried to maintain a balance for preserving the voice and stories of each person, while keeping in mind today's reader. I followed guidelines adopted by the national Oral History Association as I edited each interview, removing false starts and repeated information. At times I reorganized the sequence of some stories, making them easier for the reader to follow. Occasionally, I inserted additional information in brackets to make the narrator's meaning more clear. However, the language, words and grammar remain entirely those of the pioneer voices.

We view events through our own lenses and sometimes remember them even more selectively. This affects the accuracy of all historical sources, especially oral histories. Some, such as Leonard Paul, honed stories over the years for appreciative audiences; other reticent narrators conveyed more sparse accounts. We are fortunate that several of our voices, such as Harriet Allen, Marjorie Roberts and Bill Warren, could share their own memories and are also able to recount stories their parents told them of earlier events. Some narrators may contradict each other, while others tend to embellish, but all the voices remain true to their own experiences of Priest Lake.

We are indeed fortunate to have these interviews to draw from today. Most of these pioneers have since passed away, but because of their willingness to participate in the oral history project, their voices can still be heard and remembered. We are grateful to Kathleen Tonnemacher at the Bonner

County Historical Society who transcribed the Priest Lake Museum oral history tapes and did her best to capture the words and phrasing of each interview. Jeanne McAlexander Tomlin copyedited the narratives, attempting to maintain consistent spelling of place names and people. Complete copies of the oral history transcripts and the tapes are available at the Priest Lake Museum and the Bonner County Historical Society Museum.

"Coolin as I first remember it"

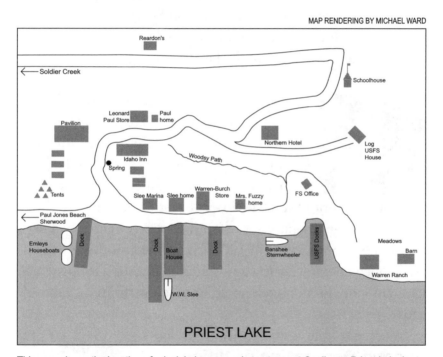

This map shows the location of principle homes and structures at Coolin, on Priest Lake in the early 1900s. Rendered from a hand-drawn map by pioneer Harriet (Klein) Allen.

Introducing Priest Lake Voices

First Generation of Voices

Leonard Paul was born in 1888 in Neenah, Wisconsin, and came to Priest River at the age of 12 with his mother after his father died. He opened a store at Coolin in 1906 at the age of 19 with the assistance of his brother-in-law, Priest River merchant Charlie Mears. Paul married Vera Moore in 1914, and they had three daughters, Marjorie, June and Betty. In 1923 he developed Paul-Jones Beach, and he opened his expanded new store in 1926. Leonard Paul died in 1971 at age 83.

Rudolph Fromme was born in Richmond, Indiana, in 1882. He received a bachelor's degree from Ohio State University in 1905 and a master's degree in forestry from Yale in 1906. Forest Service Chief Gifford Pinchot sent him to the Priest River Forest Reserve, where he became supervisor when the name was changed to Kaniksu National Forest in 1908. He worked for the U.S. Forest Service for 37 years in eight national forests. Through Leonard Paul, Fromme remained in touch with Priest Lake all those years.

Second Generation of Voices

Harriet (Klein) Allen, born in 1905, was the granddaughter of Joseph Slee who developed the first marina in Coolin. Her uncle was W.W. Slee, namesake and captain of one of the earliest steamboats on the lake. A graduate of Washington State College with a degree in home economics, she was a dietitian at the Desert Hotel in Spokane and home economist at *The Spokesman-Review*, writing the Dorothy Dean column. Married to Clyde Allen, the couple had two sons, David and Ted. The family maintained the original family log cabin located near Four-Mile Island until her death in 1988.

Russell and Mona Bishop developed the marina at Coolin in the 1940s that still bears their name today. Mona's father, Ed Elliott, operated the tugboats on the lake, and Russ served as his pilot.

Ike Elkins first came to Priest Lake on a fishing expedition in 1912. He worked for logging contractors and established his own logging business in 1929. He had garages in Ione and Newport and is said to have been the first person at Priest Lake to own a car. He was married to his wife, Susan, for 69 years and they had two daughters, Joan and Jan, and a son, Albert. In 1932, he acquired a rustic resort of fishing cabins on Reeder Bay, which his family developed into Elkins Resort. Elkins died in Florida in 1989 at the age of 97.

Ernest Grambo began a long career with the Forest Service building trails at Priest Lake in 1930 while still a senior at Mead High School in Spokane. He also served as fire dispatcher at Beaver Creek Ranger Station and Civilian Conservation

Corps crew foreman. By his retirement in 1970, he was assistant regional forester at Denver, Colorado.

Brandon "Junior" Lambert was born in 1907 in Minnesota. He came to Priest Lake in 1938 to work on Rose Hurst's ranch near Nordman.

Fulton Messmore served in the Civilian Conservation Corps (CCC), helping to construct the Luby Bay Forest Service building that today serves as the Priest Lake Museum. He first came to the area in 1930 from Los Angeles and went to work for the CCC in 1934.

Rose (Chermak) Meyers, born in 1897, grew up on her family's homestead on the Nez Perce Indian Reservation. She attended Lewiston Normal School and came to Priest Lake in 1915 to teach at the Nordman School. She met her husband, Harry Meyers, when he came to stay at his father's homestead near Nordman. Eventually, they settled in the Spokane Valley and had two children. In 1950, they bought a cabin at Reeder Bay, which later became their retirement home.

Jack Monette was born in Quebec, Canada, and came to Priest Lake in 1929 to work for the timber companies. He later developed his own business cutting poles. He also worked on Rose Hurst's ranch near Nordman.

Margaret (Calfee) Randall came to Priest Lake in 1922 when her father, Wert Calfee, established a dairy on the Warren Ranch in Coolin. She attended grade school at Coolin with Marjorie Roberts and Barry Shipman. Margaret married Frank Randall, and they returned to Priest Lake after he retired from Potlatch Forest Industries.

Marjorie (Paul) Roberts grew up in Coolin where her father operated the Leonard Paul Store. She married Jim Roberts, commander of the Civilian Conservation Corps camp in Coolin. They lived in Japan with their two daughters, Helen and Charlotte, after World War II and returned to Priest Lake to take over management of the store in the 1950s. Marjorie died in 2001.

Ivan Painter began building trails for the Forest Service in 1933 at the Beaver Creek Ranger Station. The following season he manned a Priest Lake lookout, then became a boatman. After serving in World War II, he returned to Beaver Creek until 1949 when he went to work for Diamond Match Company.

Vonnie (Austin) Smith, daughter of Edna and Herman Austin, lived for many years at the Continental Mine where her parents worked. She attended school in Porthill, Idaho, and married Charlie "Tot" Smith in 1931. The couple raised three children. Vonnie died in 2004.

Barney Stone was born in 1908 and raised in Priest River. In 1931, he began working for the Forest Service at Coolin as a packer, delivering supplies to lookouts and camps. He served in the U.S. Navy during World War II and was employed by Diamond Match Company until he retired.

William Warren was born in Hillyard, Washington, and moved to Coolin briefly in 1922. His father homesteaded in Coolin Bay and served as justice of the peace for the lake. The family lived for several years in Spokane, and Bill moved back to Priest Lake perma-nently in 1936 and established the Warren Dairy. Bill Warren married in 1941, and he and his wife, Elaine, continued to operate the dairy until 1953.

Nell (Carey) White's parents, Charles and Katherine Carey, were married in 1906 and homesteaded at the Outlet. Nell's grandmother, Martha Carey, oper-ated the Northern Inn in the early 1900s, and her great-uncle was Andrew Coolin. She went to high school in Sandpoint where she met **Bill White** in 1926. About 1945, they bought the Lamb Creek Inn from Irma Britton and operated it until 1958. Bill was captain of the Forest Serv-ice boat, *Clear Joe*, and also worked for the Bon-ner County Road and Bridge Department.

1.

CHANGING THE WILDERNESS

The train station in Priest River in the early 1900s shows the arrival of the Great Northern Railroad; some of the passengers were bound for Priest Lake via stage.

Getting to the Lake

While traveling Highway 57 from Priest River today, it is difficult to appreciate how isolated Priest Lake remained for the first half of the 20th century. The Great Northern train dropped passengers off at the tiny Priest River station where they still faced a rugged, 30-mile journey north. The original road crossed the Priest at the confluence with the Pend Oreille and then ran east of the river to Coolin. This route avoided the necessity of bridging the river or its tributaries.

Most who ventured to Priest Lake before the 1920s arrived by way of a long, uncomfortable stage ride.

Priest Lake's lack of direct access to the railroad slowed the area's development. For some, like operators of the Woodrat Mine, this meant transportation costs eliminated the viability of getting their ore to the smelter. For others, like moonshiner Pete Chase, it allowed him to exist with little outside interference. Vacationers to Priest Lake spent weeks in the summer, not just weekends, after enduring the long trek north.

1900 – Stage line to Priest Lake operating

1904 – Charles Beardmore buys stage line from Abe Lee

1914 – Stage robbed, a federal offense because it carried U.S. mail

1914 – First motorized stage purchased by Beardmore

1914 – Stanley Jones begins operating the stage line

1920 – Stanley Jones gives up stage line and mail contract

1937 – Bridge across the West Branch allows direct access to the West Side

1951 – Bridge completed to connect the Dickensheet to the West Side road

1955 – Highway 57 completed to Highway 2

HARRIET (KLEIN) ALLEN

It was a rugged trip. Everyone who was able got out and walked up the hills to save the horses, and when it was a four-horse stage, you got out and the men pushed if it got stuck in the mud. When it was motorized there were no doors – sort of leather buggy seats crosswise on a truck bed and a running board, of course, high above ground, so it was quite a leap to get up to your seat. The person on the end of the seat held on to a metal bar as you journeyed along. I don't believe we ever stopped at the Halfway House to eat after the advent of the motor, but it was a whole day trip by horse stage, and then we did stop about noon.

When it was a horse stage, we took the train [from

The original St. Elmo Hotel in Priest River was acquired by the Beardmore family in 1902. Travelers would spend the night at the hotel; the Beardmore Stage would pick up passengers traveling to Priest Lake.

Spokane] the day before to Priest River and stayed all night at the St. Elmo Hotel (salmon pink color, owned by Beardmore) right by the station. I remember Mama and Grandma, in linen dusters for the trip, pushing a bureau against the door, as the lumberjacks were pretty noisy and roistering at night. We got up to breakfast in the dining room with long tables, syrup jugs, sourdough hot cakes, coffee and bowls of stewed prunes. Mama

The Halfway House at the Prater Ranch was a stop for the Beardmore Stage. The Halfway House provided an opportunity for the weary passengers to have lunch before continuing their 12-hour day trip from Priest River to Priest Lake.

neatly shooed flies off the food as we ate and hurried out to get on the stage.

By noon we had reached the Halfway House and got stiffly off to go into a good noon meal for $1 or 50 cents. I've never had such big, round molasses cookies since. While Mama changed the baby in the privacy of Mrs. P's [Effie Prater] guest tent, I watched the men draw water from the well. It was curbed up with wood and a hook, and they would bring a galvanized or wooden pail and then a windlass. They changed horses there, and we went on to reach the lake about suppertime. It took 12 hours versus 45 minutes now.

Quite often as we came to the crest of the hill, getting the first glimpse of the lake and the Northern Hotel, someone shot off a gun to announce us. Then we went with a flourish to stop at the store and be welcomed.

Later when Stanley Jones had a heavier-type motor stage, and the roads were less corduroy and dustier, they met the train about 10 a.m. and made it into Coolin by 1 p.m., in time

The Northern Hotel, built in the 1890s, was located in Coolin at the south end of Priest Lake.

for the passengers to have dinner at the Idaho Inn. Then the steamer *W.W. Slee* took them up lake the next day. How we hung on the porch rail to see who came in every noon!

After these trucks were available, the train left Spokane about 8 a.m. and got to Priest River about 10:30. You got on the stage with your lunch basket, and when the mail and freight were loaded, we started. Soon we were on the way up a terrible hill out of Priest River, then off around turns and bends through heavy forest to stop at every mailbox or homestead. Usually someone was out to greet us or send orders to be filled next day. Many boxes were at logging roads leading back into camps. When we used to come in with Mr. Hawley, people brought their lunch baskets full to overflowing, and we ate on the way. I remember one time when Will and Mrs. Burch and Wallace, the son, came in the same day we did, there was great pickle swapping and recipes exchanged.

One day a road hog wouldn't let Stanley Jones by as he was driving the stage and the dust was deep, and they came in about an hour late all covered with dust. I remember the biting

Stanley Jones, Leonard Paul, Daddy Duffill and Paul Mears on Daddy Duffill's houseboat, in the 1920s.

sarcasm of Stan as he said, "We followed a gentleman in," and everyone was slapping dust off themselves. The luggage was just a mound under dust. This slow car wouldn't pull over or get out of the middle of the road from East River in. When Mother first went [to the lake] in the 1890s they had to lift the carriage over some stumps first, or they went in on horseback.

MARJORIE (PAUL) ROBERTS

The mail and freight came [to the Leonard Paul store in Coolin] by horse and sleigh, horse and wagon, or big freight truck, depending on the time of year and condition of roads. The Joneses had the contract when I was 6 to 12, and when they came by horse, the barn behind the small cabin on the hill housed the horses overnight, and they returned the next day. The Halfway House on the Eastside Road was where you could get dinner, and the fresh horses were hitched. The last time I ate there, I was 14, returning from school in Walla Walla for Easter. The mud was terrible. They fed me, but I didn't have any money, so Mrs. Thomas' sister, who was coming to visit them, paid for me. Dad took care of it when we got to Coolin. It took 12 hours, 6 a.m. to 6 p.m.

LEONARD PAUL

We'd start in the morning and get to the Halfway House for lunch and unhitch the horses. We'd go in and eat and then start out again with a fresh team of four horses. I remember one time Harvey Wright was coming up to the lake with us. He'd made several trips up, as he used to carry the mail years ago. Mrs. Prater was a teetotaler. So, Harvey was on the stage with a bunch of us fellows one day. When they got to the Halfway House, Harvey said, "The last time I ate dinner there, I was pretty-well oiled up, and she read the riot act to me, so I don't

Mr. Prater and his prize bull at the Halfway House.

dare go in."

"Well," I said, "you can't sit here in the stage." He was pretty well inebriated, so we picked him up and put him in the manger with hay in the barn and we went in and ate. We didn't say a thing about Harvey and the driver didn't either. When we got through we hitched up the horses and got ready to go when we realized we forgot Harvey. We went in and picked him up out of the manger and got him back onto the stage again. He cussed us and said, "Damn, you might have at least poured a quart of whiskey on that hay. At least I'd have had something to eat." Whiskey in those days was a full quart with 100 proof. He was a case, toughest guy I ever saw!

Who had the contract?

Abe Lee had it; Williams had it. You see, you buy a ticket at the Great Northern Depot in Spokane to come up to the

The Beardmore Stage in front of the St. Elmo Hotel. The stage carried mail, freight and passengers from Priest River to Priest Lake.

lake. You would buy your ticket clear through to Coolin. You get off the train in Priest River and stay all night at the St. Elmo Hotel. Next morning you get on the stage and get up here. The Great Northern would pay the stage their part of it. They had the mail contract, and they also carried the freight. They had three mails a week in the summer and two in the winter. They relayed the horses; we had horses here and at Priest River.

NELL (CAREY) WHITE

When we first lived on the homestead [at Outlet] there was no road of any kind up here. Our only way out was taking a little rowboat across to Coolin and catching the horse-drawn stage to Priest River. There was a place down in the Blue Lake area we called the Halfway House, and the teams would pull in there about noon, usually on the way out. And these people

The Beardmore Auto Stage went into service in 1914, replacing the horse-drawn stage.

named Prater [James and Effie] would have a big dinner for everybody. I can remember the long tables and benches. Mrs. Prater was a very good cook, and she'd have three or four kinds of meat and baked cakes and pies and all kinds of goodies. Everybody would eat a big meal while they fed the horses. Then we'd take off for Priest River and get in there at 6 o'clock in the evening.

WILLIAM WARREN

Dad had a freight line coming in with teams of horses and wagons from Priest River to bring the Forest Service all their equipment and supplies for those big fires [in 1910]. So to pay for taking teams back to Priest River, he had a big wide sailboat that he put a small engine in, and he would go to Woodrat Mine, get bags of concentrated ore from the mill and haul them to Coolin. Then they would put them on these wagons and ship it to Priest River where they were sent by rail, probably to Kellogg or Wallace.

The whole country in 1910 seemed to be on fire, and he was able to get the contract to supply the Forest Service everything they needed. The way it happened was they called for bids from various people, and my dad hadn't read about this until the day before. So he went to the local ranger and said why wasn't he invited to bid on supplies? He said, "Well, I didn't think you had enough buying power to handle it."

"Well," Dad said, "would you still accept my bid?"

And he said, "Sure, if you could get it in by tomorrow, the deadline." So his bid amounted to – he would supply everything for cost plus 10 percent.

The bids were opened and they called him in and said, "This is very unusual."

"Why is it unusual? I'll get you anything you need from a needle to a saddle."

Dad gave them a few phone numbers for Jensen-Byrd and grocery wholesalers in Spokane, because he had been in business there, and said just call them for reference. The next day the Forest Service asked him to come over to the office and said, "It's your contract."

So he put on a couple of teams of men to bring the stuff in. In fact, that would be in real competition with Charles Beardmore at that time, I believe. Beardmore had a freight line, but it was mainly a daily stage line coming into Coolin. The mail contract had been with several people with awfully good service, too, when you consider the weather and the roads that we used to have; why, it's remarkable the way they came through. Very seldom would you be missing the daily mail; you might get it a little late, but the mail always got there.

Since we moved back to Coolin [in 1936] there is no problem except in the spring. But in the old days, spring could be about six weeks of melt, so you couldn't get in and out. You'd fight it as well as you could, and then you'd stay home. The mail came in by a team of horses. If you had a large enough truck and do it with chains, you could probably fight your way in and out. It just wasn't worth it. Sometimes people tried to go out early in morning when the road was frosty and solid. Lots of people tried and they would come down and get me because we had a dual-wheel truck, and I would have to go rescue them. Of course, I was doing that for the neighbors, so there was never any charge. If I remember correctly, the fishing season started the first of May and they could be still fighting mud at that late date, depending on how cold it had been the winter before. I've seen some awful mud. They kept putting more gravel on the roads and finally they considered blacktop. Then in 1957, this road was completed so that we had good blacktop all the way.

Do you remember coming up here when you were young?

We'd leave Hillyard in the Model T Ford, and it would take four or five hours if we had a good run, and we'd get in for the weekend. There was no blacktop, of course. It was a ferry at Newport to come across the Pend Oreille River. And then the road from Priest River was something else. All this time my Dad was trying to buy an automobile that would come in the best and we went from Model T Fords to a big Hudson, which was considered the most powerful car on the road. We had more trouble with the Hudson than we ever did with the Model T Fords. I remember them telling stories about trying to come in with some of the first automobiles; they would find people stuck on the Jack Pines Flat. They were trying to get in for the early fishing season, and the road would be a mess.

Early Coolin

The first paths into Priest Lake led to the southern end along a narrow but accessible shoreline where, according to William Warren, the Indians camped on the beaches in the fall when they came for the whitefish. In 1890, the Great Northern Railroad built a two-story log hotel at Coolin, counting on visitors to flock there from the soon-to-be constructed rail line 30 miles away at Priest River. However, the arduous, rough-cut road limited lake visitors to mostly miners, trappers and a few hardy homesteaders.

Andy Coolin, early homesteader on Priest Lake. He was the founder of Coolin, Idaho, platted in 1907.

St. Louis native Andrew Coolin, along with family members, homesteaded the land just north of the hotel and established a post office, thus bestowing the modest site with his own name. Marjorie Roberts recalled: "Andy Coolin was kind of a wheeler-dealer of his time, from the stories that I heard. He never really settled down here to live. He'd come and then he'd go someplace else."

When Leonard Paul arrived in 1906 he remembered: "Walt Williams owned the hotel, and they called the community Williams. The name of the hotel was called Klockmann because there was a man named Klockmann who grubstaked all these fellows that wanted to go out and prospect." When Paul's mother became postmistress in 1908, the name of the town was changed back to Coolin. After the turn of the century, changes in the Homestead Act increased timber activity *and marginal improvements in the road brought more settlers and summer visitors into the area. By 1910, Coolin could boast two stores, two hotels, a marina, a school, a saloon and, just to the north, Camp Sherwood for hardy summer visitors.*

Originally named the Northern Inn, it was renamed Hotel Klockman after the developer of the Continental Mine, Albert Klockmann (his name was sometimes spelled with two N's). Today it is called the Old Northern Inn.

1890 – Northern Hotel built by the Great Northern Railroad Company

1893 – Andy Coolin becomes postmaster of Coolin

1900 – Abe Lee operates a stage line and carries the mail

1900 – Andy Coolin proves up his claim

1904 – Kaniksu Forest headquartered in Coolin

1906 – Leonard Paul opens his store

1906 – Richard Handy proves up his homestead named Camp Sherwood

1907 – William H. Warren takes over homestead at the end of Coolin Bay

1909 – Second Coolin School built

1916 – Third Coolin School built, now the Civic Center

1923 – Paul-Jones Beach opens just north of Coolin

1926 – Leonard Paul opens his new store

1942 – Idaho Inn burns down

Leonard Paul on Coolin after 1906

There was Andy Coolin's house, which is where my rose garden is, and the Northern Hotel up on the hill, and Walter Slee and two cabins; one that Wheatley lived in and the other that Tony Lemley lived in. The Forest Service buildings came later. Abe Lee and his wife were running the hotel. Walter Slee lived here just in the summer.

The Slee home at the Coolin waterfront, July 1916.

The road quit where the store is now. The first road north of the store came after I bought Paul-Jones Beach and built the road that far [in 1923]. And then [Harry] Handy got [Charles] Reardon to build the road from Camp Sherwood down to the Paul-Jones Beach. The Dickensheet was just a trail where old man Dickensheet would walk down to his cabin. When they cut that through, they called it the Dickensheet Road.

Marjorie (Paul) Roberts on Coolin, 1910s

The Forest Service had its head office for the Priest Lake region [in Coolin]. The ranger's family lived in a large log house on the hill above the office. There was a big barn out back for the pack train and a long dock with a boathouse for the launch that took men and supplies to the upper lake. The only phones in town were on the Forest Service line, one at

Edward "Dad" Moulton, on right, is shown relaxing on the beach with friends and his dog.

The Idaho Inn, owned by Ida Handy, was a destination for fashionable travelers.

their office and one at the hotel. The store didn't get a phone until the new store was built [in 1926] and it was also on the Forest Service line.

The Warrens owned the ranch in the bay, but when World War I started Mr. Warren moved out to sell meat to the army and didn't move back to Coolin until the 1930s. Wert Calfee ran the ranch then. Mrs. Calfee baked and did washing for the Forest Service men. There was the two-story Northern Hotel on the hill. The owner decided to go to Alaska so Mrs. Handy bought it.

HARRIET (KLEIN) ALLEN ON COOLIN, 1910S

My mother told about the first time they came in the horse and buggy. They had to lift the buggy over the stumps. There was just a slashed-out road, really an Indian trail, because the Indians were the first ones who came in, principally for fishing, hunting and the berry season. This was sort of a campground, I guess.

Swimmers in early 1900s Coolin. Edith Phelan, Harriet Klein and Mrs. Fuzzy in the water.

The road ran down from the top of the hill and schoolhouse, past the Northern Hotel and two or three small houses, and then past Leonard Paul's Store, set into the lower hill. It swung past the covered spring in front of Mrs. Handy's hotel, The Idaho Inn, and stopped at Grandfather Slee's cabin beside which stood two storage sheds or warehouses with a boardwalk in front. Slee's had a long dock and slip for their rental rowboats and later motorboats; also a repair shed and the steamer landing.

There was a rival store on the beach next to Gramps [Slee]. The first owner after Clarence Burch was Mrs. Gorsline. Then came Mrs. Fuzzy who lived in a neat-as-a-pin little cabin down the beach a few rods south with her mother, Mrs. Bear. The restaurant had an Edison Victrola and a few records, which were heard nearly all day and night. Folks sat around over a beer or coffee, and occasionally young people danced a bit. In front of the store was a dock with the *Cliquot Club*, Burch's houseboat, and often the Jack Schaeffer houseboat. To one side was a small boathouse for their launch.

When you followed a woodsy, green trail down a few hundred feet, you came to Mrs. Fuzzy and Mrs. Bear's neat little cabin and next to it a small one-room house of some sourdough. The path wound up a small hill and out by the Forest Service office building and the Warren Ranch. Just above was the ranger's log house. The Forest Service had a boathouse and a dock in front of the office. In front of Mrs. Fuzzy's cabin, the old two-deck *Banshee* had run aground in the mud and stayed.

A few small tent houses were scattered here and there on various levels. Mrs. Handy had a large dance pavilion and a few small tent houses for guests. Later, Paul-Jones Beach was developed and more houses were built from Coolin to the Point.

Out the road where the schoolhouse sat at the crest of the hill [now the Civic Center] by turning left, one came to Abe Lee's small cabin, now Lee Creek Road, which sat by the creek running into a small pool overlooking a meadow. Lee was tall, looked like Lincoln and fairly quiet. About one mile was a farm and lovely meadow called the [Charles] Reardon place, always a favorite walk in summer to call on Mrs. Reardon. They raised lots of hay and furnished milk to the community, as did the people who lived on the Warren Ranch at the foot of Coolin Bay.

The Idaho Inn in Coolin showing tent cabins for overflow guests, early 1900s.

MARJORIE (PAUL) ROBERTS ON THE IDAHO INN

The Idaho Inn had a lobby with a washroom, pitcher and basin, and coat hooks on the side. The dining room was large, four- and six-person tables, and two private rooms on the end for parties or family dinners. She had two little offset arched rooms in the back that were private dining rooms. It was really quite something, you know, to go into a private dining room. I don't remember having a menu. The food was excellent, white tablecloths and pots of honey and hot biscuits with each meal. The second floor was all guest rooms. Then the attic probably had a couple of rooms where the help lived.

Mother Handy was a motherly looking woman and had very heavy white hair, very efficient. She was a business-woman, ran both places and did her own cooking. She had a nice three-room apartment in the back of the inn, right off the kitchen. She had one daughter and one son, Harry and Ruth.

Dad [Leonard Paul] and Harry [Handy] knew each other in school in Priest River. So Mother Handy must have lived in

The Idaho Inn in 1942.

Priest River at some time. Harry went to India and had a carnival. He'd come home every two or three years, and took his mother around the world one time. When World War II started, he got caught in Bombay and just got out with his skin. The year before he had sent his wife, Tiny, home. She was an Australian bareback rider in his circus when he married her, and she couldn't get into the United States. So Dad did

The Idaho Inn burned to the ground during the winter, circa 1943.

some vouching for her and they got her in through Canada and into the states. Harry owned Camp Sherwood and Tiny lived there until she died.

Dad took us out about once a week to teach us manners when we were small. And [Ida Handy's] big deal was home-made biscuits with honey. The honey was always on the table, and the first thing you were served was hot biscuits, and then you could get your dinner. The honey was Priest Lake honey made from fireweed. Different lookout guys used to take the hives to the lookouts in the summer and then bring down the honey. We used to sell fireweed honey in the store.

The social life of Coolin centered around the hotel or the school. Many a box social took place at the hotel. The kids were piled on a bed and someone played piano and someone fiddled. Grandpa Moore was a popular fiddler. Mrs. Handy built a restaurant across the street with a large front porch overlooking the lake and an inside dining area. There was a back room with two pool tables and a lot of gambling went on there, run by Art Marston.

Art Marston helped Mrs. Handy around the place and had his own sawmill across the bay from Coolin. He was her live-in, but in those days no one called them that. There were a lot of shack-ups in those days and most old sourdoughs had what they called "a long-haired cook." One summer, Mrs. Handy hired a cook who married Art. Mrs. Handy was so upset, she fired her and kicked Art out.

Mother Handy had a good chance to sell and decided that all she wanted was the restaurant. The hotel was sold to the Hodges and they ran it till it burned down in 1944. She never lived up at the Great Northern; rented out that hotel or got somebody else to run it for her. The house Mrs. Elliott used to live in, that little one on the corner, Mrs. Handy

The Art Marston sawmill across the bay from Coolin at the outlet of the lake.

lived there after she sold the hotel.

Mother Handy died in 1924, I think. They called Mother [Vera Paul] down, and she was there all day when Mother Handy died, probably of pneumonia. People often called Mother to help out because she was always at home, for one thing, and she had a pretty good supply of medical things. Not that she had any medical knowledge especially, but she had a lot of common sense that way.

WILLIAM WARREN ON THE IDAHO INN BURNING

The Idaho Inn burned in the wintertime during [1942]. The mail was quite late coming in that day because of bad roads. Went back up later and this thing was burning, so I helped to take a piano out of there, slipping and sliding through the snow. Of course, all the water for fire protection was shut off because it was wintertime, and they had to get the pumps going at the store. They had a pretty good fire system but it was all drained for winter.

The Art Moore home next to it, a little low house, was saved from burning although it broke a lot of windows from the heat. My dad came to see what was going on and stood around a corner of Art's building with a hose, which wasn't putting out much of a stream. But when the hotel finally burned out and fell into it, luckily, it saved Art's house. Everything had been moved out 'cause it was so close.

[The Idaho Inn] had years of paint that had been put on to clean it up each year, you know, and a lot of wallpaper that burned for quite a while. It was a hot fire. I never did hear what started it, but every once in a while you'd hear a bullet go off inside when the heat would reach them, but nobody was hit. Finally it just got to where we had to get away from it and let it burn.

HARRIET (KLEIN) ALLEN ON SLEE'S MARINA

I still remember Grandpa [Joseph Slee] puttering around the docks at Coolin singing, "I'll take you home, Kathleen." He had two acres in Coolin he bought, probably from Andy Coolin. He built a small log cabin facing the dock and boat sheds; front room, combination bedroom and kitchen, with a large storehouse next to it, and two large log boat storage sheds. Later, behind the log house, he put up a two-bedroom rough board house for the family to use during the summer.

At the end of the dock, riding magnificently on the gentle waves, was the gleaming *W.W. Slee*, a steamer built to fit the lake trade. The front half was enclosed to carry freight and keep people warm and dry in storms. The boiler was in the center and the woodpile on port side. The pilot seat and big wheel were on the starboard with two doors on each side, one to let people enter and one for loading wood. Walter Slee steered the boat from the seat with a window (like the cab in a

W.W. Slee Marina in July 1916. Rowboats were for rent, and rides could be purchased on the steamboat at the Coolin docks.

locomotive) to lean out.

Uncle Walter, W.W. Slee, had polio at the time of the Spanish-American War, which left him helpless from the hips down. However, he lived to be 50 and made a fine life for himself transporting people on the lake, first in a steamer the *Kaniksu* and then in the steamer *W.W. Slee*. He was a gentle, handsome man, and everyone loved him. I can still see those pistons going up and down, with the oil cups filling with a greenish-brownish oil from a long-spouted oil can, with the rhythmic thud of the engine and the ripple of the water as the nose of the boat cut a clean, furled furrow, and the wake followed.

The back half of the boat was covered from sun and rain but open on the sides for a clean view. Seats back-to-back gave room for about 10 or 12 out there. The gangplank rode on the front top and was pulled down at each stop as swaggering youngsters ran down to the beach. The older ladies carefully picked their steps and gratefully held the hand of the handyman, who also carried off freight and mail to the eager groups

Harry Bear, Windy Bill and Walter Slee, who is at the wheel of his steamboat.

that were always gathered on the beach to wave us in and off.

Every winter Grandpa Slee would build one or two rowboats or double-enders [at his home in Spokane]. They would come up on the Great Northern when he came up in the spring. Mr. Bigger would carry them up [to the lake] on his lumber wagon. Each spring he added a couple of boats, and sometimes during the summer he built one or two. Pretty soon he had quite a few rowboats to rent, different sizes, different widths – different ideas about what fishermen wanted. The term "double-ender" means they came to the point at each end. They think of rowboats nowadays as straight at one end that has an outboard motor, and the other end is the pointed part.

LEONARD PAUL ON SLEE'S MARINA

Slee finally got Evinrude motors. They were the first outboard made; had a spool on top and you cranked it. Never forget the time Gus Larsen – he was a professor at Moscow – took up these lots around Cape Horn. He came here on his honeymoon, got his groceries and went up there. About four or five days later he came down at the store with his wife. He was swollen up and he couldn't talk or anything. Course like me, I had to laugh and said, "Well, that's a fine way to treat your husband on your honeymoon. Did you use a beer bottle or a rolling pin?" So she had to tell me what happened.

It was a cold morning. Gus was tuning up this engine. He was a big fella, and he had his overcoat on, too. The damned thing backfired, that spool hit him on the jaw and knocked him clean out of the boat. He went down to the bottom of the lake like a ton of bricks, and she just laughed her head off. But the truth was that the cold water brought him to, and he got out all right. Well, they sold their place and moved back to Iowa and he is still there. Used to hear from him quite often.

Marjorie (Paul) Roberts on Moore's Marina

One of the big deals at the end of year was to get everybody on the *W.W. Slee* and have our school picnic on an island. It wasn't a passenger boat; it was a tugboat-type thing. It had a big back end and you just sat out there or in the front end. In between were the motor and this boiler and there was a walkway, just hardly that big to go from the back to the front. It didn't go very fast. It went chug, chug, chug.

Slee's house was a low log hovel. The docks always looked like they were breaking up, and the covered slips were half there and crooked. He had old wooden rowboats and Evinrude motors. The joke was that none of his motors ever ran long enough to get you back home. The *W.W. Slee* was parked at the end of the wharf. The Winslows lived in a float house on the other side of the dock. Bert Winslow ran the *W.W. Slee*.

Art Moore was Mother's brother, and when he came back from World War I, he had his own marina. And then, eventually, he bought out Grandpa Slee. Grandpa Slee had the first marina. By the time of World War I was over, the only boats Slee had were little rowboats. And the buildings had all collapsed on the end of the dock. In fact, the only thing Art bought was Grandpa Slee's old cabin after he was gone. But there was a guesthouse behind his cabin, and Art and Mary lived there. The docks were still there and the old buildings and all, but Art bought the property, and that's how he got started and stayed until he died in 1956. Let me see, he built the [current] marina around the mid-1940s and sold Chris-Craft speedboats.

Before Art went away to war, maybe after he came back too, he worked for the Forest Service and ran the Forest Service boat up and down the lake every day. It was what they called a launch. Had a big motor in the middle of the boat and you sat on the side around it.

Art Moore Marina in 1932. The Moore Marina used the old Warren-Burch Store on the right for storage.

Sam Byars had a dock and a launch that went up lake every day, and he had a barge. He was the one that would barge stuff up and down the lake, and he owned Forest Lodge at the head of the lake. Load the barge with lumber; a lot of the cabins were built that way, and that's how they got the lumber and other materials up there.

The original Leonard Paul Store built in 1906, with Paul Mears, Leonard Paul and daughter Marjorie.

Leonard Paul Store in Coolin

In 2006, the addition of Wi-Fi for laptop computers at the Leonard Paul Store heralded yet another generation that claimed the store's front porch as the heartbeat of the community. A hundred years earlier, folks gathered on the store porch waiting for the delivery of mail by the stage. A Priest Lake institution today, Leonard Paul established his store at Coolin in 1906 at the age of 19. His brother-in-law, Charlie Mears, and his mother, Amalia Paul, helped him set up Priest Lake's first real general store in a 20-foot-by-30-foot log cabin. Since all access to the lake was through Coolin, Paul's store quickly became a vital hub to the whole region. His inventory reflected his customers – the trappers, miners, hunters and vacationers – who stocked up on provisions before heading up lake. In 1926, Paul built the current store a little north of his original log cabin. Paul operated the store into the 1950s, admonishing customers, "If we don't have it, you don't need it." Like his store, Leonard Paul himself became an institution as he *witnessed Priest Lake's transformation from wilderness to bustling community, thus serving as a reminder to newer generations of the area's rich legacy.*

1906 – Leonard Paul establishes store at the age of 19

1908 – Amalia Paul becomes Coolin postmistress because Leonard is too young

1914 – Leonard Paul marries Vera Moore

1915 – Leonard Paul officially becomes Coolin's postmaster

1926 – Log store replaced with the current building

1948 – Paul's daughter and son-in-law, Marjorie and Jim Roberts, join Leonard operating the store

1965 – Jim Roberts retires as postmaster and post office is moved out of the store

1970 – The Roberts sell the store to Ken and Rosalind Brown

1971 – Leonard Paul dies

1977 – Store changes hands to Ken and Allison Delf

1978 – Store is purchased by Gordon and Diana Hudson

2005 – Pat and Teri Akins become new owners

LEONARD PAUL

Charlie Mears said, "How'd you like to start a store at the lake?" I said that would be fine. "Well," he said, "let's get her going before winter comes." So he contracted with Tom Benton, who had a homestead on the Eastside Road. Benton Creek is named after him, and he was Mrs. Prater's father. Old Tom built this first log store, which was 20 feet by 30 feet inside. I think the price was $300 or $500, and I was to furnish the windows and doors. Well, he did, he built it so I came up with old man Littman who was a carpenter there in Priest River, and it was during Thanksgiving time. We slept in the kitchen of Andy Coolin's shack, which was right next to the old store. We ate up at the hotel and put in the counters, shelves and one thing and another. Then I went back to Priest River and bought my opening stock. Charlie Mears helped me with that. In the meantime, after Dick Mears dissolved partnership with Charlie, he went to Spokane and started a dray line. He delivered stuff like pickup trucks do today, and we got Dick to haul my opening stock up here during the winter. Mother stayed in Priest River all this time until I got settled up here. Anyway, I opened the store on the 15th of February in 1906.

We had to pay a cent a pound for freight just to bring it up from Priest River. A barrel of gasoline would cost me five dollars and a half freight just to get it up here. I didn't have gasoline then, but I bought coal oil in a 50-gallon barrel. A sack of flour cost 50 cents more than it would in Priest River just for the freight on it. So, just like it used to be in Alaska, if you bought anything you bought the very best. Instead of a case of peaches weighing 60 pounds in two and a half size cans that were maybe a dollar cheaper than the very best, you buy the best because the freight was the same. And that's always been the case in out-of-the-way places. You get a better grade of stuff than you would back in town. No use paying a lot of freight on something that isn't very good.

HARRIET (KLEIN) ALLEN

Coolin was only a cluster of log or board and batten shacks [in 1910]. The general store run by Leonard Paul was rather new, a solid log building, the rear set well into the bank of the hillside with a long wooden porch about wagon-step level across the front. At one end you entered a standard door to the store half with two long counters, a post office cage and marvelous glass display case on one counter.

Large double doors opened at the other end of the porch to the warehouse and storage area. Name anything you needed and he had it. Tin pants for loggers, boots, socks, thread,

needles, screen, water pipe, lamp chimneys, crocks for sourdough and dill pickles, flat irons, lanterns, Hershey bars, gum,
hairpins, canned peaches and tomatoes, beans, rice, sugar. Coffee was in large metal boxes to be ground in a fierce-sounding
coffee mill and poured into a bag. Of course, coffee beans sold
to you to take home to grind fresh each day.

Crackers were in square metal boxes, flour in huge sacks, salt
in smaller sacks, sugar in 100-pound sacks, Log Cabin syrup in
little tin log cabins, pink round peppermints or hotter white
peppermints, rope in coils, nails in kegs, stove pipe and sundries.

But the peak of the day was when Mother Paul would
come in with the fresh loaves of bread from the oven – big,
fluffy brown loaves – some already ordered and some for a
lucky chance buyer. She and Leonard lived in rooms behind
the store, and later he built the first unit of his present house
higher on the hill and separate from the store. We were always
sure of going there for dinner at noon on one of the days we
spent at the lake each summer. She and Grandma Slee were
dear friends and we looked forward to her visits at Grandma's
in Spokane. You could never forget the meals Mrs. Paul
cooked, nor could you hardly move from the table – such fra-
grant light rolls and jam, tasty German touches to the vegetables and huckleberry or apple pie.

Marjorie (Paul) Roberts

The store was a log building with a full-length porch. The
main front part was divided in half – main store with a long
counter on each side. The right side was full of groceries: a coffee mill, scales, cash register and a big wheel of cheese. The
back was lined with shelves full of canned goods. The left
counter had a glass showcase with tobacco and tobacco cutter,
and candy. The back shelves were full of dry goods, gloves, sus-

penders, long johns, bootlaces, bandannas, all for men. I don't remember any lady things.

There was a potbellied woodstove near the back and on the left corner a table and cubbyholes for the mail. The other half of the front of the building was a warehouse. It had a large screened-in portion, floor to ceiling where all the sack goods were kept: flour, sugar, rolled oats, beans. This was to keep the mice from eating through the sacks and spoiling things. The other half was full of canned goods. There was a small office off the post office corner.

The back of the building was one large warehouse full of buckets, brooms, washtubs, gas cans and such. There was a screened box also where the ham, bacon and smoked sausage hung from the ceiling. If the meat got moldy it was cleaned with a vinegar-soaked rag. There was also a large barrel of vinegar, and you brought your own bottle to fill. Outside the back door was a bench with a washbasin, dipper and pail of water. Coal oil was pumped from an underground tank.

Bread came from the Priest River bakery in a large, square wooden box. It held layers of 1-pound loaves, about 24, I guess. Next day it went back to be filled again. Bananas came once in a while. They were in big stalks and hung from the ceiling on a rope with a pulley to keep them high. I remember seeing two tarantulas in these stalks. We got them this way up into the early 1950s. The store carried dynamite stored in the back shed, roofing, cement, glass, rope; anything not carried was ordered up from Priest River. No fresh milk, eggs, meat or vegetables. Most people had their own, or you got it from those who did. Boxes of candles were common and coal oil lamps, later Coleman gas lamps. By the time I was 6, we had lights in the house and store from a carbide plant. The front of the icehouse had a room where the plant was. Dad poured in the carbide pellets and filled it with water once a week. The light wasn't much more than the lamps but much cleaner and no oil smell.

The waterfront at Coolin showing development, including two hotels, two stores and a marina.

How did goods arrive at the Leonard Paul store?

It came by whoever had the stage contract at the time – the mail contract but other stuff, too, at the same time – and it came to Priest River by rail. And he bought lots of his stuff by boxcar – buy a boxcar full of flour. He couldn't buy a little bit, and the flour came from clear back east, so he'd buy a boxcar full of it. Then maybe he'd split the boxcar with somebody in Priest River or maybe some farmer may take five or six bags for the winter. So by the time he got it up here he had storage room for it. But a lot of the stuff was brought by boxcar.

He'd have to buy it six months ahead. He bought for next year. If you didn't have your order in by the first of December, you didn't get it and then they delivered it just as soon as the roads permitted. All of our wool jackets and everything, we got those in April to be delivered in September. And tools and especially things like that – tools and his candy orders – he sold lots of candy. Especially Bunting candy. Bunting was the brand name and he had it shipped out from Chicago. A

The Leonard Paul Store carried a variety of merchandise.

whole big shipment of candy would come in the spring of the year, and he'd get rid of it by fall. When one of the bachelors was invited to dinner, he always took a box of candy to the hostess. I don't remember candy bars in the early store. I do remember stick candy and licorice type candy and horehounds and that type of thing.

Why did he decide to build a new store?

Well, the little one was just too small. There just wasn't any room, and it was just one of his dreams to build a modern store. So in '26 he built that building with the dance hall up-stairs. He wanted to make a dance hall, kind of a recreation place for people. He had an architect by the name of Thompson, Noel Thompson, who was George Hill's uncle. He's worked on a lot of big buildings in Spokane. Dad told him what he wanted and that's the way it came out. People thought it was going to be just huge and we'd never be able to fill it up. Dad said, "Well, for once I got it big enough," but you know it never was big enough.

Were there a lot of changes when they moved from the old building to the new one?

No, the basic change was people – there were more and more, especially children, as the roads got better. There were more salesmen who came up here to sell. You didn't have to go finding them; they found you. And then, as time went on, the different companies started to deliver, some once a summer or every month or every week. But I can remember when we first came home, we would get three pop deliveries a summer.

LEONARD PAUL

Did you ever sell fresh milk in the old store?

No, I don't remember when I started selling fresh milk. We used to buy canned Carnation milk in 50 case lots, and sometimes when you cut the can open there would be a big chunk of butter in it from traveling. Warren and Reardon was the first ones to peddle fresh milk, then Thomas would peddle milk. Then Bill Warren started to supply milk to the store but, hell, they couldn't supply enough. It was all in bottles then and that was a nuisance.

You must have had to keep it cold some way?

Well, we had ice, ice boxes. They used to put up ice here,

at the cookhouse, at Paul-Jones Beach and at the hotel. Four places kept them busy all winter. A lot of times we went out to Chase Lake 'cause it wasn't thick enough on the lake. There was one year I had to go way down to Diamond Lake to get ice. You want to build an icehouse with a lot of cracks in it so it gets air, then put your sawdust all around it and tamp it good. It was hard to shovel off the ice and chop out a chunk and then horse it in. Chunks weighed 200 pounds the way we cut them.

When I moved from the old store [in 1926] I had so gall-darned many invoices and stuff that I burned them all. I burned everything that wasn't up to date, and I shouldn't have done that. I had that old set of books where you would take an order in the order book first, then you filled it, checked it off, transferred that into a day book, then from the day book you carried it over into the ledger. At the end of the month you'd make an itemized bill by dates and everything; one package of yeast – 5 cents, pound of coffee – 35 cents, and so on. I'd send customers a statement of everything they bought. Well, it was a big job, but that was the way we did it. When National Cash Register put out that file (large cash register) we are using today, I bought it and that made it simple.

LEONARD PAUL ON GETTING THE POST OFFICE IN 1908

Finally, along came the post office. Tony Lemley had it, and he didn't want it. He said to hell with it after the inspector came up and gave him hell about Mary taking the stamps because she didn't think it cost them anything. He gave up. Records show he didn't do much business anyway. We still got his records. Well, the inspector said you'd better pick out a postmaster.

I'd worked for the post office in Priest River and didn't want to monkey with it. So old Charlie Horton came down

Built in 1926, the second Leonard Paul Store featured an upstairs dance hall that attracted large crowds in the summer.

every three months from Eight-Mile Island to cash his check. He'd go to the hotel and pay for a night's lodging and a breakfast and supper the night before. Then he'd come to the store and buy what he needed and cashed his check. If he had any money left, he'd go to the saloon and drink up the rest of it. Next morning he'd go back up lake. Well, he was a pretty smart old codger. So the rangers and all of us were at the saloon one night and Mac said: "Why the hell don't Charlie take this post office? This pays a little and he knows enough to run it. He knows a lot more than Tony does." So we put it up to him. He said he didn't want to monkey with the post office. So we got him drunk and finally got him to say "yes," he would, so we all went to bed happy. Next morning when he picked up his stuff and started up lake, he says: "Leonard, I changed my mind. I don't want it."

I told the rangers because they were the ones that were pushing it and they said, "Why don't you take it?" I told them I

The Coolin Post Office was located in the store for many years.

wasn't old enough. Well, they said, your mother could. She lived here with me. So we'll make her postmistress, and you run the post office. Well, I finally agreed because it wouldn't pay the stage to run without that mail contract. Mother signed her name to all the reports and everything. I put all the junk in the wheelbarrow and moved it down to the old store and started up.

The postal service kept piling it on, and we got money orders, but mother always had to sign her name. When the Civil Service was established, I said I would take the Civil Service examination and be postmaster. I had to go to Sandpoint to take that examination, and you had to have the authority that they sent you. I forgot to bring my certificate to get in and was afraid I couldn't take the examination, but an attorney said he'd fix that. So I explained what happened and took the exam. I didn't get a very good grade, but anyway that's how I became postmaster.

The Leonard Paul home, built in 1906, was attached to the original Leonard Paul Store.

MARJORIE (PAUL) ROBERTS ON THE PAUL HOUSE

You could get a drink at either of the hotels. I know Dad always had a gallon jug or two down in the store right under the counter. If somebody came off the lake and wanted a drink, all he had to do was set out the glass and they got some. I don't remember him selling it, but he always had a glass with a friend. Everybody came in for the mail periodically. They didn't come every day, but when they did come they tried to make it during the mail so they'd see somebody, if nothing else.

There was just an old potbelly stove, what we used to call a camp stove like you've seen in bunkhouses in camp. And they just sat around on breadboxes because [bread] came in a huge wooden box, 20 loaves. If you wanted bread, you opened it up and took a loaf. They sat on the breadboxes; they sat on cracker barrels; they sat on the counter, but there were never that many at one time.

Dad built his first house when they moved to Coolin, and he and Grandma lived there. After he decided to get married, he enlarged and modernized it. And it's the same house, but it's just been added on to. The original part was the kitchen, and what is now the dining room was the living room, and then there was the bedrooms on the back. And, of course, there wasn't any plumbing, but there was a woodshed.

The water tower was always there. After Mother died, he put up the second one, a red cedar tank he ordered from Seattle. Dad would pump for two hours from 12 to 2 o'clock. He furnished water to the whole town, and he would pump for two hours and everybody would draw all the water. They would bucket it and draw it off and that would drain the tank, and then the next day he'd do the same thing. We could never have water in the wintertime because it would freeze.

We had a cow and, oh, sometimes we'd take a couple of pigs and butcher them in the fall, but we didn't have pigs all the time. We had turkeys. They were silly things, and we always had ducks and chickens. When we were teenagers, [my sister] June had to have a horse. So Dad got a horse that was so swayback that June was the only one that ever rode him. Dad just tore the first store down, but they moved the building where he used to keep the dynamite up the hill. That little log cabin beside Tom Moar's house was once beside the store.

Mr. Warren had a store on the lake where the parking lot for the marina is now. A family joke was that when he walked past Dad's store, Dad rang the cash register several times to make it seem as if he was closing a big sale. The [Warren] store was later sold to Mike Moore, who ran an ice cream parlor there.

The *Slee* at Lionhead with the *Kaniksu* in background. Rowboats were loaded to take passengers and supplies short distances.

Getting Around the Lake

If the trip from Priest River to Priest Lake was a challenge until the late 1910s, getting north of Coolin required even more effort. After the turn of the century, steamboats in summer provided transportation around the lake. However, most residents relied on rowboats. Harriet Allen recalled, "There were no outboard motorboats so unless you were 'rich and influential' and had a launch or inboard motor, you rowed everywhere in light, double-ender cedar skiffs or heavier and deeper rowboats with one or two pair of oars." When Rose Meyers came to teach school in 1915, she was met in Coolin by Johnny Walker, who rowed her all the way up lake to Reeder Creek. It was the Forest Service and the timber companies who first turned the trails into roads around the lake, though both still relied on lake transportation well into the 1950s.

1892 – A small steamboat operates on Priest Lake

1904 – Joseph Slee's *Kaniksu* provides service around the lake

1907 – Cecil Wheatley builds the paddle wheeler *Banshee*

1914 – Freight line begins from Priest River to Reeder Creek

1914 – Settlement at Reeder Creek gets post office; recognized as Nordman

1919 – Bridge over the Upper West Branch completed

1925 – Construction of the Dickensheet Bridge begins

Joseph Slee's steamboat, the *Kaniksu*, provided service around the lake in 1904. It is shown here with Walter Slee at the helm.

LEONARD PAUL

The first steamboat here was gone by the time I got here [in 1906]. A fella named George Bartoo built it; that's who Bartoo Island is named after. I never saw it; I don't know what happened to it. He was already gone, just like Dickensheet, Cavanaugh and Hess and all those old-timers who were here before I came.

Slee built a little boat and made regular trips around the lake when I came. People come in on the stage with their tents and would go up lake to camp at Granite Creek and Canoe Point, all over the lake. He would take them up there, and every day he would call on them, get their orders. He did a good business.

HARRIET (KLEIN) ALLEN ON THE *W.W. SLEE*

My grandfather, Joseph Groton Slee, and his family, used to come up to camp, hunt and fish, and go up to the Thorofare. They bought some land from Andy Coolin at Coolin, right where Russell Bishop's Marina is, built a cabin and a large warehouse where they could store their stuff from year to year. They'd come up on the train [from Spokane] to Priest River, get on the stage [to Coolin]. They got a boat then so they could go up to the head of the lake.

From that developed the business they finally end up with – the steamer that carried passengers and firefighters and whatever else was needed from Coolin to the head of the lake every day. If anybody ordered a catch of logs, they took the logs. Some other men came in with one or two tugs afterwards; they worked better with the logs.

They'd go up the lake and somebody would say we got a lot of huckleberries or they are out of sugar and would you bring some when you come back, or would you see if we have any mail. Because, you see, there was no way into the lake or around the lake except to go by road to Coolin. And there were no roads on the other side – either side – you came to Coolin. Then you had to go up the lake some way. There were dugouts and lots of small boats, but at first there weren't any outboard motors or anything of that type. Later, there were one or two launches and a small steamer that they brought in.

There was a substantial wooden wheelbarrow to take all the goods and freight to load families like the Hungates, who camped on Canoe Point; Gus Heatfield, who had a cabin across on Tripod Point; or the Bob Hall family, who stored camping gear in Grandpa Slee's storehouse. It was brought out and put on the steamer when they arrived for their vacation – small, sheet-iron camp stoves, roped tent rolls, camp cots, buckets, axes, shovels. People really camped in those days – blackened coffee pot, kettles, skillets, white or blue enameled cups, plates and bowls.

About 8:30 a.m. there would be a warning whistle and then soon after a farewell toot, and the steamer would back out of the slip with real deep chug-a-lugs and then square away on a straight course for Four-Mile Island, cutting a clean swath and leaving a big bubbly white wake. The pistons would go up and down and the deep-throated chug and smell of hot oil and the crackle of the logs burning in the boiler firebox were a part of the center of the boat where Bert Winslow stood with one foot in the open door where they loaded the wood. Uncle Walter would be at the wheel in his seat by the window where he steered, or could reach over to adjust gauges and pressure at the boiler. Six or eight people would be on the rear deck. Two benches back-to-back made seating, or there was a broad gunwale and upright posts to hold up the roof and many chose to sit there and look out at the water. A small toilet room was just at one side, built back in the wood box.

The first stop might be Four-Mile where Katherine Burt and her mother were at a long dock. She was very attractive and there would be cheerful calls and jokes, with mail and supplies put off and lists picked up. Then on to Hunt Creek where the McCreas and Veaslys and Dr. Nelson and Jim Ford's sister had cabins. On up that side to "Little Rosalia," just where the channel between Eight-Mile Island and the Horton Creek Point came, all the Palouse families would come down to the gangplank or, on the other side, the Vinther-Nelson cabin on Eight-Mile. Then we'd go slowly through that deep cut and on up to Plummer's at Indian Creek, a lovely sandy beach with few people except their house and the Forest Service station.

Then we backed out and went around Pinto Point to where Johnsons and Wadhams and the Harry Bears had places, on around Cape Horn, which was always rough, to Granite Creek and from that stop to the Lone Star Ranch of Harry

Angstadt's on Bear Creek. His wife, Belle, had a large goiter and popping eyes and was quite a big woman.

From there, we went to the [Mose] Fish's place at Twin Islands, then came Canoe Point, Bottle Bay, Huckle-

The *W.W. Slee* made daily trips around the lake, leaving the Coolin docks around 8:30 a.m., and returning about 4:30 p.m.

berry Bay, Squaw Bay where Nig Borleske, famous Whitman coach, camped, perhaps over to Beaver Creek to the Forest Service Station, then to Mosquito Bay or Lionhead Point and docked for lunch. It had no dock though, just a gangplank, and no other people except who we brought with us.

Byars had some cabins, and doctors or lawyers came there. Guiding was a business to show where fishing and hunting was best in those days. Geisingers were at the Thorofare entrance to the little lake as you go out of the channel near Dad Moulton's. "Frank the Finn" lived in a float house at the head of the little lake – didn't like many people, very poor.

The Thorofare entrance to the Upper Lake. Daddy Duffill's float house is shown with Forest Lodge across the water.

About 1 p.m. we had loaded wood and started back and went to Reeder Creek or Kalispell Bay or Luby Bay, as the need called. Then back by 4:30, unloading those we'd picked up, mail to go out and lists for Leonard Paul to fill. People often rented rowboats and were towed behind the Slee to their campsites. What wilderness!

Never will the forlorn picture of a young schoolteacher from Boston fade. She had a small trunk and two "telescopes" (they are wonderful suitcases made to swell up as you filled it and used leather straps to hold them together). At Reeder Bay, a man had come from Nordman to pick her up in a lumber

The *Banshee,* the only double-decker paddle wheel boat on Priest Lake. Its final voyage in 1911 occurred while carrying supplies to Upper Priest Lake, when it hit a rock in Kalispell Bay.

wagon. The bay and beaches made a lovely sandy crescent. There were no houses on the water then, but a wagon trail came down to the lake, and Uncle Walter delivered to the people who lived back in the woods and campers along the beach. Later, a road from Priest River to Nordman made a stage possible for mail and supplies.

Trips on the *Slee* were made daily, leaving Coolin at 8:30 a.m. and returning about 4:30 p.m., with an hour out to re-fuel and eat lunch at Mosquito Bay, where later Nell Ship-man had a camp for movies. But for years it was lovely and quiet; Lion Creek went just to the south so we'd hike over to see it, clear and rippling and green, picking huckleberries as we went and teetering over a log to get to the other side of the creek and back. Often a small boat, towed, would take stuff over to Sam Byars on the Thorofare or go up to the little lake to the ones who lived there – Cougar Gus, Pete Chase, Dad Moulton, Old Frank and "Stinkfoot

George" – or tourists who wanted to see what the Thorofare
meant or what the little lake looked like.

LEONARD PAUL ON THE *BANSHEE*

[Cecil] Wheatley built the *Banshee* so he could get through
the Thorofare. He had a homestead up at the head of the lake,
you know, the little lake. He was going to make a town out of
it. I've got a map of it, all platted and surveyed. They called it
the town site of Wheatley. There were no roads on the west
side, so he built this big boat. It was 60-feet long with a 20-foot
beam and a flat bottom.

He bought a team of horses with a sled so he could get his
stuff up [to Coolin from the railroad in Priest River]. He built
the boat here, and the first time he had it out was on the
Fourth of July. Paul Mears was up here with me at the time,
and the saloon was up on the hill. We sat around in the shade,
and every little while we would send Paul up the hill to get
some beer. We talked Wheatley into giving us a ride in the
boat that night.

We had our fireworks and firecrackers, got the girls from
the hotel, and loaded the boat, a double-decker. Well, we
paddled the lake, a moonlit night, drank the beer and shot the
firecrackers. Paul put a bunch of small firecrackers down Carl
Burch's neck. And, Jesus, we had a hell of a time pulling his
shirt off, but he wasn't hurt. There was just a little chunk of ice
left. One of the girls from the hotel was on the other end of
the deck; they took the chunk of ice and slid it down the deck
and hit her in the heel. She went down like a ton of bricks
and, Jesus, she was mad. Well, to make a long story short, we
got up as far as Bartoo Island and Wheatley said we were out of
wood – everybody should go ashore and get wood. He said,
"You want to go to the head of the lake, don't you?"

I said, "How far can you go?"

He said, "About six miles farther with what we got."

So I said, "Turn her around and take us back, to hell with getting wood for this boat." So he did, and we got back without having to get off and get more wood. That was his big trouble; he never could put enough wood on that tub to get to the head of the lake.

It had a great big steam boiler and a big paddle wheel, full width of the boat. The boat was all right and you could go through the Thorofare, but he finally wrecked it on Indian Rock. He had all the winter grubstake on board that I had put up for those homesteaders back of Reeder Creek. And he had a big load besides.

Instead of going around the island like he should have, he went through the channel there by Linger Longer. Well, you know that rock, they have it buoyed now, but if there is just a little ripple you can't see it. He slid right up on that thing; knocked a big hole in the bottom of his boat and there she hung. Well, of course, the water came in and spoiled all the flour and sugar and other stuff. Finally they shifted the load

Dad Moulton on Thorofare.

Upper Priest Lake near Thorofare.

and slid sideways off the rock. He took the [wet] flour and put it over the hole. He got back down here, but it was a mess; had to fill their orders all over again.

HARRIET (KLEIN) ALLEN ON THE *BANSHEE*

The *Banshee*, a stern-wheeler, had gone aground and settled down on its haunches in the mud and sand in front of Mrs. Bear's and Mrs. Fuzzy's cabin. At first we children loved to climb all over it. It was a two-deck, rather open job and for a long time we could turn the big steering wheel on the lake side and take long, imaginary trips. The benches were on the upper deck and it had part of the boiler and engine, but bit by bit it disappeared. The ice broke up the lower part and finally it was no longer an attractive nuisance.

MARJORIE (PAUL) ROBERTS ON THE *BANSHEE*

The *Banshee* was the one and only paddle wheeler on the

lake. And the reason they couldn't keep it going up and down the lake [was] they couldn't keep enough cordwood to keep it steamed up. They had cordwood at the different islands where they'd stop and load up, but it just took too long and too many people cutting wood. I never saw it except where it was beached in front of what was then the Fuzzy's cabin. And we went swimming there as little kids 'cause it was a nice sandy beach and no docks around and we'd jump off that old *Banshee* 'cause it was grounded there. It was disintegrating every year, but then in World War II when they had a scrap metal drive, that was the last of it. The town went together and got the old boiler and all the old scrap.

Early pioneer Thomas Kerr's family, Pearl, Lloyd, Lealiah and John Marquette Sr.

Mose Fish homestead. Mr. and Mrs. Fish are shown in front of their cabin in 1911.

Homesteading at Priest Lake

The Homestead Act of 1862 opened up the West to settlement, but it was not until the 1890s that homesteaders began claiming land around Priest Lake. To obtain 160 acres free from the federal government, Priest Lake pioneers had to locate unclaimed land that they could farm or ranch. They filed a claim with the U.S. Land Office in Coeur d'Alene and then had to live on the land for five years, clearing it and improving it with buildings. If homesteaders could "prove up," they received a patent that gave them title to the land.

The promise of obtaining free land in the West by farming often proved a struggle, but it was especially daunting around Priest Lake because of the isolation, rugged terrain and short growing season. One couldn't survive by farming alone, so successful homesteaders needed to find another means of earning a living while proving up. With each change in the Homestead Act, Priest Lake experienced a new wave of hopeful settlers. In 1906, the Forest Homestead Act released additional acres from the reserved forestland deemed to have agricultural potential. In 1912, laws changed to allow homesteaders to prove up in three years instead of five because much of the remaining land in the West, like that around the lake, was marginal for agriculture.

After proving up, a few Priest Lake homesteaders like the Reardons near Coolin or John Nordman near Reeder Creek were able to continue farming their land. Others like Andy Coolin and Cecil Wheatley schemed to divide up their homesteads for real estate sales. Some like Richard Handy, with land on the lakeshore, developed commercial ventures for summer visitors. Today, many of the lake's place names are a reminder of those early homesteaders who first settled the region; among them are Coolin Bay, Kerr Lake and the Nordman Post Office.

1862 – Homestead Act

1898 – Priest River Forest Reserve opens up to homesteading

1898 – John Nordman files for his homestead on Swede Flat

1900 – Andy Coolin proves up his homestead at the south end of the lake

1906 – Forest Homestead Act

1906 – Richard Handy proves up at Sherwood Bay

1908 – Cecil H. Wheatley proves up at Trapper Creek in Upper Priest Lake

1906 – Swan Hager proves up near Reeder Creek

1912 – Homestead Act of 1912

1917 – William H. Warren proves up in Coolin Bay

LEONARD PAUL

When I first came here, Sam Byars helped to locate these fellows [on homesteads]. Take a fella in Spokane who wanted to take up a homestead, he'd give Sam $100 to locate [land]. Mike Sherman got Sam to locate them over on the west side, where the Sherman's ranch is. Others like Abe Lee, Reardon,

Albert and Hellen Hagman with their son Clarence on their homestead in Snow Valley, south of Priest Lake.

Claude Reams and Jim Davis all just picked out their homestead and proved up on it.

But in those days a fella couldn't make a living homesteading; he had to go to work. Everybody prospected and they'd trap and they got by pretty good. And, of course, when I first came there was more Civil War veterans here than anybody else, and they only got $36 every three months. They lived on $12 a month, a pension.

You couldn't take up a homestead unless the land was more suited for agriculture than timber 'cause this area was all Forest Service at that time. They'd survey all the timber off and give you nothing. Of course, [Priest River National Forest assistant] Rudy [Fromme] did go by the book. For instance, if a person applied for a homestead, he would send out a surveyor and if there was a clump of good trees on this quarter section, they'd survey around it instead of giving the homesteader a square 160 acres or quarter section which he was entitled to. They wouldn't allow many trees. So all of the plats in the early homesteads up here are cut up like a jigsaw puzzle.

Winslow homestead on Reeder Creek. Shown here are Mrs. Bert Winslow, Graydon, Grandpa Mead, Dorothy and Bert. The Winslow homestead is the site of the current Elkins Resort.

There wasn't any women here then until the homesteaders brought in their wives. If a fella wanted a wife, he'd get a Heart in Hand book from Michigan, write a couple letters and then go down to Priest River to meet her and bring her up here and marry her. Old man Handy was a justice of the peace, so he could marry them.

RUDY FROMME ON THE FOREST SERVICE MONITORING HOMESTEADS

I contested a Spokane schoolmarm's right to patent an excellent body of white pine. This claim was in the new west side addition to the old Priest River Forest and the trail to the small summer cabin was impossible except on foot. In her statement of good faith, she wrote that she had cleared and cultivated several acres and that she kept two horses on the place. My finding, in company with one of the rangers, disclosed no clearings except a couple of small, natural openings of swampland, not exceeding an acre all told; no cultivation except a small, weedy flower bed; and no evidence whatever of any livestock, present or past.

When faced with this report, she admitted to the land office judge, or registrar, that she had only visited the place several times as a summer outing, generally in company with her gentleman friend, and that her reference to horses merely meant "two sawhorses," which they had used in construction work and which she thought were still there. I believe our protest was sustained.

Lewis "Pete" Chase and Leonard Paul enjoy a shot of moonshine.

NELL (CAREY) WHITE ON HOMESTEADING AT THE OUTLET

My father [Charles W. Carey] came to the lake before my mother. His mother [Martha Carey] had a hotel at Coolin called the Northern Hotel. She ran that hotel for a number of years, and my father lived with his mother. Met my mother who came to Priest River to teach in 1905. They were married in 1906, and at that time he decided it would be a good idea to homestead a piece of property at the Outlet. [The homestead] went down the lake to the mouth of the river and down the river to what is now Highway 57, and extended across that highway and up the hill a short ways on the other side. He built a little log shack – still standing. It had three rooms in a straight line, a living room, a bedroom and the kitchen.

WILLIAM WARREN ON HOMESTEADING COOLIN BAY

Cal Huff came in and started to homestead this property [at the end of Coolin Bay] many years ago. But Cal was told that his property was on a school section. The survey hadn't been completed yet, and he could never homestead a school section, so he moved down on the peninsula at Priest River and homesteaded a farm that later became one of the better farms of the area.

My dad and mom first came to fish. They had never heard of Priest Lake before they proceeded on in here. He said the road was so bad that even with good horses and a good buggy, if he ever got out of here alive, he'd never come back. But when he got to the lake, he fell in love with it. And there was

Shown here are Pete Chase, Bob White, Frank Algren, Frank Brown, "Cougar Gus" Johnson, Maude (Whittaker) Collier, Dick Collier (desk clerk at Davenport Hotel). Pete furnished his moonshine, *Uncle Pete's Monogram*, to the Pennington Hotel, which in turn sold it to the Davenport Hotel during Prohibition. Maude was the organist at the Orpheum Theatre in Spokane.

a man who was homesteading this piece of property and had marital trouble, so they bought his interest in the homestead.

When Dad originally homesteaded, he understood that he only had to stay one year. So after a year's time, my folks tried to prove up on the homestead. They spent all the money they had saved up and hired people to help clear the land and things like that. And then they were told it was no longer the law, that they now had to stay a full five years. So that's when my father went to trapping and also opened a store down on the beach known as Warren and Burch [in 1907]. He was able to prove up after five years, then went to Spokane and back into business in 1912 or 1913.

The original homestead cabin remained on this property until 1933 or 1934. My family put a lean-to addition on the side. We got water from a spring out back of the house, like everybody did. One morning [they] went to get their buckets of water and found a dead chicken in the spring. So they sent out to Priest River to get some drainpipe, which was an inch-and-a-quarter wide by 5-foot length, and a pitcher pump and a

Dad Moulton was one of Priest Lake's early hosts. He is shown here with hunting guests.

sand pump or a well pump. They started driving this point and the water hit the ceiling of the lean-to, and that was the first artesian flow that anybody found around here. The original well still runs. We have put in additional wells, of course, and furnish water service to other people from the artesian flows but with pressure systems now. That water was used for many years at the Warren Dairy to cool the milk.

They cleared considerable land, tried to develop springs and drain land, and so forth. It was just a case of trying to make a living on it. They built a barn and improved the little cabin. There was a root cellar, for one thing, and a wood cellar in the barn, a little cabin and a chicken coop or two. Oh, you had to have a woodshed and an outhouse, of course. The root cellar was built on top of the ground with sawdust for walls. The sawdust was hauled from the little mill across the bay from Coolin in boats and gunnysacks and stuck in there. Of course, it was also an icehouse in conjunction with the woodshed.

WILLIAM WARREN ON HOMESTEADS

First there was the township of Coolin, homesteaded by Andy Coolin. That's where it got its name. It was Abe Lee that had a homestead over at Lee Lake, which would be east of here. The next thing going north from Lee was a [Charles] Reardon homestead. Then there was a [Sam] Davis homestead and then a [Claude] Green homestead. There were four of them in one line in that valley. North of Coolin, there is another homestead, the [Richard] Handy's place. Then there was a [Pete] Chase homestead out by Chase Lake.

Abe Lee lived in the East, came out here looking for peace and quiet, and he homesteaded. I don't know whether he had income from other sources or not, but he pretty well lived off the land. He was a big tall fellow, a very quiet man – lonely, like most sourdoughs, as we called them in those days.

LEONARD PAUL ON HOMESTEADS

Bill Shurr's homestead was where the upper river comes down into the little lake, a lovely property. Trapper Creek comes down where Pete [Chase] used to have his still, and there is enough water there to provide electric lights to the whole town site. That is where Dad Moulton had his Kootenai No. 2 mine, that tunnel and shaft. The Geisingers' homestead was [at the foot of the little lake]. They had silver fox; they sent way back to Maine for breeding stock to start with. They had to move out, couldn't make anything there.

MARJORIE (PAUL) ROBERTS ON HOMESTEADS

The Winslows had a homestead where Elkins [Resort] is now. It was one of the main stops for the supply launch from Coolin; the ranchers from the Nordman area came there [to meet the boat]. Across from Granite Creek, on the east side, was the Lone Star Ranch. It was a halfway house for those walking or rowing from the Upper Lake. You could get a meal, fresh baked bread, eggs or milk.

The Fentons [had a homestead in Cavanaugh Bay] and they lived there, probably a stump ranch at the time. He did odd jobs for people, Mr. Fenton did. But they had a cow and some chickens so people going up lake could stop there and get milk, eggs and cheese. And I heard a lot of people say, "Oh, we used to go down to Fentons' and get bread." Where they lived is now where the airport is. And then Rex Sutton bought it from them, and he put in what you might call a resort. He's the one that put in the boathouse, storage and the store. He had a little restaurant there at one time and cabins to rent.

The Mitchell Mine claim, tunnel No. 509, in 1904. Shown here are Bill Brawley, Bob Gumaer and Leonard Paul at age 16.

The Continental Mine. Pictured is the Glory Hole, which was where the outcropping of ore rich in lead and silver showed above ground. Albert Klockmann, developer of the Continental Mine, learned of this site from the Indians who used lead found here to make reloads for the rifles purchased from Hudson Bay Company.

2.

MAKING A LIVING

Miners First

For generations, Kalispel and Kootenai Indians made their way to Priest Lake in the summer and fall for the abundant whitefish, but historians maintain they rarely stayed year-round. As in much of the West, miners were the first white people to stay throughout the winter and attempt to make a living at Priest Lake. In the early 1890s, profitable discoveries in the Coeur d'Alenes to the south prompted miners to scour what

The Continental Mine situated near the Canadian border on the Blue Joe Creek, north of Upper Priest Lake and west of Bonners Ferry. In 1922 the township of Klockmann, shown here, supported a population of 350 people.

The Continental Mine, rich in ore and legend, was discovered by Billy Houston and developed by A.K. Klockmann with help from Spence Smith and others.

is now Bonner County looking for lead and silver. A.K. Klock-mann claimed one of the most dramatic and successful mining ventures when he established the Continental Mine north of Upper Priest Lake in 1890. He developed the mine over several years; at first attempting to bring ore out by way of Priest Lake, but soon focusing on a more practical route over the Selkirk Mountains to Bonners Ferry.

The mine remained productive until World War II. At its height in the 1930s, the Continental employed more than 200 miners who, with their families, lived in the adjacent town of Klock-mann. No other mine around Priest Lake became as profitable, although miners persisted into the 1930s, leaving the lake's shore

The upper building, tunnel No. 1, at the Continental Mine.

pockmarked with tunnels and tailings. Some mines such as the Nickel Plate near Nordman, the Mountain Chief on the Upper Lake, or the Woodrat near Luby Bay generated much anticipation but yielded only modest shipments of ore and few profits.

1890 – Continental Mine established

1906 – Superintendent appointed at Nickel Plate Mine

1910 – Woodrat Mine ships ore

1914 – Jared Mitchell develops Mountain Chief Mine

1915 – Continental Mine mill destroyed by fire

1916 – Dad Moulton displays copper ore from his Kootenai 2 Mine

1916 – 100 miners employed at Continental Mine

1920 – Andy Coolin working Woodrat Mine

The following two observations reflect the contrast between published accounts of the Continental Mine's beginning and the oral tradition. Today, histories of the Continental Mine

generally give Billy Houston credit for the discovery but acknowledge A.K. Klockmann for its development and success.

Vonnie (Austin) Smith on the Continental Mine

The Indians told Billy Houston about an outcropping of ore on top of a mountain in North Idaho, so he went up in the hills and located it. He didn't have money enough to stake it and have the claim proved up, so he thought about Spence Smith, his friend that lived over on Pend Oreille Lake. Spence agreed to stake him the money he needed, and they both went up and staked the mine. They went in by Priest Lake. They built a cabin right close to the outcropping. When they got some ore out, they hired a man by the name of Bailey to pack it out. There was a trail down Boundary Creek, and it was closer than down Priest Lake way, so that's the way he rawhided it out, by packhorses.

Later A.K. Klockmann came here. He was interested in mining, so Uncle Spence Smith and Billy Houston sold the mine to him. Uncle Spence got $10,000 for his interest. Billy didn't want money; all he wanted to do was trap and fish and run around in the hills. Klockmann furnished him a cabin for the rest of his life. Billy had a cabin at the foot of the hill, just above where the Continental road takes off from the foothills. One time when he was up in the hills, Klockmann had some of his men clean it out and burn it, and moved him up in a house Klockmann's brother built on a bluff overlooking the Smith Creek Slough. Billy was really mad.

Klockmann took over the mine around 1890, I think. Around 1920, Klockmann was running out of money, so he leased the mine to Bunker Hill Mining Company of Kellogg and they run it until 1928. Bunker Hill took millions of dollars worth of ore out of there in the seven years they had it. A man by the name of [Truman] Higgenbothen took over the mine in the 1930s. He pulled out all the big pillars Bunker Hill left to hold up the mountain, and it started caving in.

I was in the second grade. That winter they sent Dad down to the flume camp as foreman, so Mom went there to cook. She hired a lady whose husband was working at the mine to take care of us kids the rest of the winter. When school was out, we went to the flume camp. Mom cooked there until they closed down in February of 1928.

They had school the next year at the mine and a teacher came in. Soon after, a man came up to work. He was there about a month or so; then one day he said to the teacher, "You're going with me." He was an FBI man, and the teacher was an escaped convict. The FBI man was watching, and when he figured out he was the man he wanted, he sure broke up the school; then they had to send the kids to Bonners Ferry to school. The next year, 1923, Dad bought a little one-room house Len Shelly built at the flume camp, they hired a teacher and we had a school there until 1925. Then we were sent down to Smith Hill to school.

Priest Lake Mines and Wonders
Originally published in *The Kootenai Herald*
Kootenai, Idaho, January 16, 1892

Mr. A. Klockmann, the popular Sand Point saloonkeeper, has returned from a three weeks' trip in the Priest Lake country. He is interested in eight different locations in that section, and to find out the actual condition of his prospects was the incentive, which induced him to make the trip, at this time of the year, hazardous trip. He gives a very flattering report of the condition of the mines and anticipates a great rush into that district next spring and summer. On his various interests he has four men employed, two working steadily on one of his claims and the other two doing assessment work on the others.

From the claim on which he has the two men employed he has had assays made which have gone as high as 95 ounces in silver and a large percent lead. The vein is 15 feet wide, well defined and can be distinctly traced the whole length of the claim. He is down about 20 feet in a shaft and has started in on a tunnel.

The main lake is about 30 miles long and seven or eight miles wide, then there is a narrows of about three miles which connects the big lake with a smaller lake about six miles long, and all around this water, ledges are found running into the lake, making it a convenient place to work a mine on account of the advantages the water gives the miner in the way of getting in his supplies and in case he has a paying mine, in the freighting of his ores.

There is a small steamboat there, which does quite a business. Klockmann, who was at the upper end of the lake, just got to the landing on the day the boat made its last trip for the season, the water having frozen over during the night and next day. Had he missed the boat he would have had to walk about 25 miles on snowshoes to the lower landing. As it was he had to come out on snowshoes, taking two and a half days in making the trip.

Between 50 and 75 men are putting in the winter there, most of them trapping and hunting so as to be able to work their claims next summer, and those who are more fortunate and have outside backing are working on their locations.

Mr. Klockmann says a wagon road will be built from Sand Point to Priest Lake, a distance of 40 miles, early in the spring and that will greatly facilitate the getting in of supplies and consequently tend to bring the place more prominently before the public.

From a scenic point of view it is one of the grandest spots on American soil. Untrodden by the foot of the white man, the game from all the surrounding country has congregated there, as a last hiding place, making it the finest place in the world for the sportsman. Wild, weird and awesome, the most daring of hunters will hesitate before penetrating the depths of the Priest Lake country.

Sourdoughs

As early as 1892, more than 50 men endured brutal Priest Lake winters, hunting and trapping in order to survive while working their mining claims during the summer months. For the most part, these men were the last of a Western tradition. As railroads, electricity and automobiles brought about the modern age, Priest Lake's isolation still gave haven to displaced Civil War veterans, restless Midwesterners, reticent northern European immigrants, and folks looking to leave a past behind. These some-

"Cougar Gus" Johnson is said to have earned his nickname from skinning a cougar at the end of Main Street in Sandpoint. This early sourdough lived on a float house and worked with Nell Shipman's productions.

times-colorful residents were known collectively as "sourdoughs" for the yeast starter they would nurture, often for years. They would add flour and water to the starter to make biscuits or pancakes but always reserved a portion back to keep the starter active. Some sourdoughs like Abe Lee actually proved up a homestead, but others like Pete Chase or Dad Moulton squatted on plots of land around the lake. While searching for a mine that paid off, they survived on their yearly grubstake along with hunting, fishing and foraging. What little money they earned came from trapping, moonshining or providing day labor.

A trapper's cabin with skins and traps hanging from the porch.

1900 – Abe Lee carries mail to Priest Lake, often using snowshoes

1916 – Idaho, Washington and Oregon go dry as state prohibition laws take effect

1917 – Dad Moulton killed in gun accident

1919 – Miner Jared Mitchell dies

LEONARD PAUL ON SOURDOUGHS

These fellas could stay all winter because they lived there. Like old man [Jared] Mitchell – he'd go up lake, you know, with his supplies and [it would] get dark, he'd stay there overnight, then go up to the head of the little lake next day. Mitchell did his mining. They could walk down on the ice, but they usually grubstaked enough to last them through. They could get meat and fish all the time.

Dad's Roost, home of Edward "Dad" Moulton on Upper Lake.

MARJORIE (PAUL) ROBERTS ON THE SOURDOUGHS' GRUBSTAKE FROM THE LEONARD PAUL STORE

[The sourdoughs] would come down to get a grubstake. They'd get a sack of flour, a sack of beans and rice sometimes. There in small sacks was jack-salts, rolled oats, or something of that nature. It was only in gunnysacks; there weren't any packaged things. They'd take a case of canned milk and all the basics. I don't know if that stash would consist of a slab of bacon; our bacon was all in slabs.

The trappers would come down in the spring with their winter's catch and [Leonard Paul] had contacts with New York and houses back east that would take the furs. He sent

John Peterson portrait

Edward T. "Dad" Moulton was a prospector and hunting and fishing guide. He came to the West as a guide for General Custer and found his way to Priest Lake in 1898 where he lived to his last days.

[furs] off because then they'd get a grubstake. They never took their money home. It was left there; he [Paul] deducted the grubstake, and the rest was on credit. And the next time they came down, they drank that up and that was it.

About twice a year is all [Paul] ever saw these guys. They'd bring down marten, and beaver was real good, and they'd usually have a mink or something else, too. They brought them strung with a piece of rawhide through the eyes of the pelt and here was four or five or six pelts. They'd put them in a gunnysack and tie 'em up and put a tag on them. That's the way they did it.

Several guys up there would pick huckleberries for sale in the summer. You wouldn't believe the boxes [for shipping huckleberries]. They were cedar shake boxes, square, and they held ten pounds of berries each. If you shipped more than that, they smashed. They just brought them down, like stacked up, and [Paul] sent 'em express to Priest River [where] they went

Pete Chase frequently entertained visitors at his cabin on Upper Lake.

on the train to the Davenport Hotel [in Spokane].

Dad Moulton was one of Dad's special [friends]. He thought he was pretty neat because he said he was such a good host. And old Abe Lee, he said he was such a good host. I mean, anybody that would stop by the cabin, they were always welcome. He had constant stew on the back of the stove, and he'd whip up some biscuits and they were always welcome.

There was always somebody that Dad said, "that crazy old fool." It was usually because they'd done something stupid or gotten drunk and fell in the snow bank and never gotten home. Dad would have to go out and get a bunch of guys to carry the guy home and start his fire so he didn't kill himself. Sourdoughs would come in [to Coolin], blow their whole check and then couldn't get home with all that whiskey they were drinking and they'd fall by the wayside.

And those old moonshiners up lake, I've been in their places; they didn't even have floors in their cabin. It was just a dirt floor, and the cabin was just barely [high] enough so that adults didn't hit their heads. And the beds would be built against the wall; just boards with a mattress or springs, or whatever they had there. There was a shelf with a wash basin and a pitcher of water, or a bucket of water and a dipper, and a stove, a table, a couple of chairs or benches, and a couple of pegs on the wall to hang your gun and your jacket, and that was just about it.

Toasting the end of Prohibition, 1933.

LEONARD PAUL ON SOURDOUGHS

Old Pete Chase used to pick his huckleberries, put them in quart jars, put them in a gunnysack with a rock in it and sink them to the bottom of the little lake; had a rope on, you know. I was up there one time and he says, "How'd you like some fresh huckleberries?"

"How you getting fresh huckleberries this time of year?"

He went down, pulled up the sack and grabbed a jar, and they were just like fresh.

MARJORIE (PAUL) ROBERTS ON MOONSHINING

There was a lady whose husband was head clerk at the Davenport, and Dad and Mother knew them. And that's where most of the liquor went; moonshine came down the lake. The same guys that were picking huckleberries were making the moonshine, and they'd send down so many kegs or bottles.

I don't say that the Davenport was the only one that was getting it, but I do know for a fact that it was Pete Chase. His specialty [was] to take it to the Davenport. He'd get himself arrested about the first of November so he could spend the winter in jail. And then he'd come back on the stage, and Mother would have him up for lunch. While his boat was being fixed and ready to go, he'd say, "Well, I'm back from college." He always said that.

He wasn't little, but he was rather short. He was a funny little fellow. He lived up there [Upper Priest Lake] all summer and sent down huckleberries and made whiskey, but he'd get himself arrested periodically. There was a man named White up there too, and several others that I don't remember that well. Revenuers would go up lake in the boat and, of course, you could hear a boat coming for 20 miles. So the grapevine would get there before they did. If they did want to be found, they'd be found. But if they didn't want to be found, they didn't find them.

LEONARD PAUL ON SAM BYARS

Sam Byars had a boat, too, but his was a gasoline engine. Sam [was] coming down lake in the fall, and he didn't get here. They went looking for him, and he was dead in his boat right there at Bear Creek. He must have had a heart attack, and it kept going until it ran out of gas. It was full of kegs of whiskey. Had a 50-gallon barrel in it, so these fellas brought it down here. Elmer Stone was in on it. He was doing the distilling, and they had their setup where Sam's hotel was, going up the Thorofare in the woods someplace.

WILLIAM WARREN ON GUIDES

Fred Chant had a little rowboat at first, and took people out fishing mainly. I don't think he was a hunting guide, but he was quite a fisherman and took people out in his little rowboat.

I think several of the natives around here acted as guides occasionally, but I don't know if we had any licensed guides at that time. But most any of the natives could tell you where to catch a fish and take you out on the lake. Occasionally, some of the doctors or people with better means would come in and go cougar hunting with fellows here that had dogs, and sometimes they'd go out and kill a deer.

Log booms near Kalispell Island on Priest Lake as seen from Lookout Mountain.

Logging

At the turn of the century the large timber companies, which had reduced forests in Minnesota and Wisconsin, now vied for the resources of Bonner County. After restrictions on the Priest River Forest Reserve were modified in 1898, the timber industry gradually expanded farther and farther into the lake region. The Diamond Match Company of Ohio especially prized the area's white pine used for stick matches, a necessity before electrical appliances.

Fire danger and lack of adequate roads forced timber

Rogene Fuher works at an old-time sawmill.

crews to work during the winter months when the ground was frozen. Early logging camps literally ran on horsepower, with teams used to skid the logs through the forest. Timber companies, big and small, built logging camps around the lake that employed hundreds of men during the winter months. Some, like the Dalkena Lumber Company, used houseboats that could be moved around the lake, depending on where their crews were cutting. Others, like Charles Beardmore, built long low bunkhouses that housed dozens of men through the grueling winter.

The steep terrain and abundant streams allowed crews to build flumes, sometimes miles long, to move the logs down to Priest Lake. Companies branded their logs and stored them in booms along the shoreline until steamboats such as the E.H. Harris and the Tyee towed them down lake to Coolin Bay. During high water in the spring, men who worked the river drives sent the logs down the Priest River. These "river pigs" would push, prod and dynamite the logs for the next two months, driving them to mills along the Pend Oreille.

Log flume. The flume was a V-shaped trough into which water was diverted to transport logs to the lake.

1897 – Priest Lake Forest Reserve established

1898 – Sawmill built in Priest River

1901 – First log drive down the Priest River

1917 – Dalkena Lumber Company dams Kalispell Creek for driving logs

1923 – Tugboat *E.H. Harris* towed largest boom, 2 million feet of logs, for Dalkena

1923 – Bill Whetsler heads up the Priest River log drive for Beardmore

1949 – Last log drive down the Priest River

Harriet (Klein) Allen

Schaffer-Hitchcock Lumber Company loggers took a houseboat up to Granite Creek or stored it in Coolin as men logged back in the hills and sent large log booms down the lake. Diamond [Match] came in and logging roads opened up. They opened up the road as far as Cavanaugh [Bay] first. It was quite

Logging with horses across a corduroy road.

a beautiful road, lined with cedar and tall trees. As more logs came down, they got it opened as far as Hunt Creek and then as far as Indian Creek. It was all done in short stages. Offshoots from it were roads that came in where the cabins and the bays are, where they brought the logs down from the mountains and dumped them in the lake. Then they were picked up into booms and taken over to the mouth of the river.

Dalkena Lumber Camp No. 7; a two-horse load weighing 70 tons is shown here.

WILLIAM WHITE ON LOGGING

When I first come up here, I was a youngster; I learned to set in the sawmill on these carriages that cut the lumber. Setting, they have a carriage that runs back and forth on a track and they have a saw that runs in a circle. Put the log on the carriage and they run it back and forth through the saw, which cuts the lumber.

The Diamond Match had a mule up here at the Outlet, and they didn't have any setter above, so they asked if I'd come and set. So I took the job of setting up this mule crew.

In those days they'd go up like Caribou Creek, which is in the middle of the Thorofare, and back in the mountains and build a flume. It's a V-shaped trough with water running in it. At that time, they used horses that skidded these logs and rolled them into troughs. At the head was a little dam at this flume and they'd go by water. They'd push these logs into the Thorofare. Most of the logging in those days was done in the wintertime.

On the *Tyee* with Mr. Elliott, we was bringing the logs down from Mosquito Bay and Huckleberry Bay in a boom around half a mile long and a quarter mile wide and it would take two days. [It was] a day and a night [or] two days and a night to take those logs to Cavanaugh Bay. That's where they load them on trucks and haul them out of here.

Horse skidding. Horses were used to pull logs from the forests where they were cut.

Jack Monette on Logging with Horses

I come to Priest Lake in 1929. Times was tough then, and I come to Priest Lake looking for work; I had been making poles. When I bought my own stumpage, they were my own poles. I sold them and hired the hauling or hauled them myself, took the poles to pole companies and sold them. I had as high as six men working for me on Goose Creek and I had some on Cabinet Creek; I had my own horses, big Belgians, then Percherons.

I was on Cabinet Creek for 10 years, then moved to Goose Creek. That's about 25 miles from Priest River and about 25 miles from the lake. My brother and I worked together on the poles and we'd make 12 to 15 poles a day apiece, 25 to 30 poles a day. We'd cut them, trim them, and peel the bark off some. I had as high as six buildings at Goose Creek and there was never more than two men in one building. I got a lot of poles; the Forest Service said 70,000 poles a year. That was a lot of poles.

I hauled to Priest River and sold them. Most of the time, the farmers would come and buy 'em off of me. [The horses'] job was to hook onto the logs and drag them with the ends, follow them and take the logs to the landing. They was well trained, but they all learned so fast. You'd tell 'em to go ahead, back up, go ahead, and they'd miss a few, but go ahead when you told them to. And if you told them to swing gee and haw, they'd swing gee and haw. Gee being to the right and haw would be on the left, and they got to understand that if you trained them. The way I trained Polly, I pulled on the left line to train her haw and all I had to say was haw, and she'd turn left. If gee, she'd turn right. They get to where they understand it.

Jack Monette on Logging Camps

The living conditions wasn't as good as they are now. They had big camps and maybe 75 men or more in camps with

Dining tables at a Priest Lake camp.

different [house]boats. They didn't have no locker rooms. Later they got washer rooms and better accommodations for the camps, like they have now.

They had good cooks because I cooked myself. I helped in the camps, that is to wash dishes, clean pots and help the cook. I'd have to start pretty early in the morning, by 5 o'clock, to get things ready because the men had breakfast about 6. And then at 7 o'clock they all went out to work, so that left me. We cooked dinner for the bunch and they'd come in. The ones that didn't come in, [I] made a lunch for them and [they] would eat on the job. But the ones that could come into camp, they come for dinner at noon hour.

We'd play tricks and play the violin and other instruments, and the likes of that. That was the entertainment we had – no weekends off. We stayed there five and six months at a time in the camps.

What would happen to someone if they were in a camp and were hurt?

They'd have to take them to the hospital the best way they

knew how. They'd have to take them with horses unless they found better transportation, like cars and stuff like that. They took me in from the Panhandle Camp one time, Camp 11, into Ione when I got hurt. A horse swung and hit my leg and it hurt. That's the way they took me in, with horses; that's all they had for transportation.

Ike Elkins on Logging Camps

I used to work in the cookhouse in the winter. Back in those days, you had big logging camps and the cookhouse was large. There was a big woodstove, then a heating stove. I'd usually have to keep our fresh meat and stuff like that out in the meat house, unless it got too bad.

They'd have long tables and they'd sit on these benches. Then they had what you'd call flunkies, and that is the job I used to do. The cook would cook up a bunch of hotcakes and cover 'em over to keep warm until the crew would come in. And, of course, everybody wanted to have the first hotcakes. They usually served awfully good meals, lots of pastry, meats, potatoes and all that good food. It was supposed to keep you working on account of men were working hard –10 hours in those days. If they had to pay board and you didn't feed them pretty good, they'd get to crabbing about the meals. The cookhouse made a difference in keeping the men satisfied.

[Breakfast was served] usually about 6 o'clock in the morning. In the wintertime, it's dark then, and the men had quite a ways to walk to work. They were supposed to walk out and back on their own time. Sometimes, if they was working quite a ways from the cookhouse, then they'd have to bring out meals at noon. The first year I worked in the woods, about eight miles this side of Priest River, we used to take meals down there.

Logging camps provided hearty meals for hungry workers to keep them happy.

All these men boarded; the building they lived in was a long, long building. And they built double bunks, a lower bunk and a top bunk. They was about 5 and a half feet wide, and two men had to sleep each bunk. They had straw for mattresses, or hay. And we had to pack our own blankets; the company didn't furnish no blanket. Then they had a big stove that sat about the center of the building. A bull cook, he stayed up at night and kept a fire in this stove and waked us up in the morning.

Every guy had to do his own laundry in a tub. They had a commissary and they carried some shoes, clothing, socks, snuff – things that the men would want to use while they were there. They couldn't get out to the stores. And when you wanted anything, you'd go there and get it and they'd put it on your account. As long as you had it coming, you could draw from the commissary. Then when you quit, they paid you up in full which you had coming.

Either at Newport or Priest River, they had a small hospital. The company paid this doctor a dollar for each man that worked, and there was no insurance. If anybody got hurt or

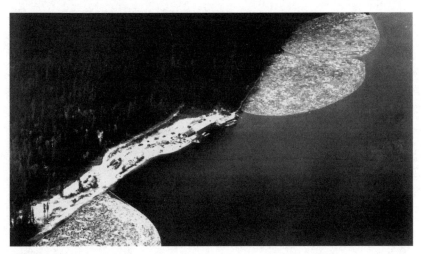
Two log booms as seen from the air.

sick, they'd take him down there at the little hospital and that's where he was taken care of.

The woods foreman got about $100 a month and board and room. [A good sawyer's wages] depends on how much timber they cut. They were paid so much a thousand, and it all depends on how much timber they cut and how good a stand of timber they were working in.

Marjorie (Paul) Roberts on Log Booms

They'd go up to the head of lake [with the *Tyee*], and they'd put these logs in the water all winter, and in the spring of the year they'd bring 'em down in great big booms to the mouth of the river. They put 'em over there in the Coolin Bay, across where the old mill used to be. And they'd tie 'em up at various places and then they'd take one and let it go, and take another one. You can see some old pilings still over here where they'd tie up a boom or two waiting for a chance to put them down the river. And when the river got to the certain height in the spring, they'd let 'em loose and down they'd go.

A 1910 river drive at the outlet of Priest Lake.

Russ Bishop on Towing the Booms

We came here in 1946, and at that time they were still towing logs up here. *Tyee II* started in 1944. It was 80 to 81 feet long, about 18 feet wide. Steam power had about 150 pounds of steam. Fire would smoke a cord of wood. The reason they did steam was the fact it was the cheapest. The war was on and they couldn't buy all new stuff. Captain Markham and Willard Bend couldn't get a permit to build a new boat, so they jacked up the whistle and built a boat under it. Some of the equipment came out of the original *Tyee*. We had the captain, a fireman and a deck hand. Everybody took their turn doing this and that. We'd get a tow and start down the lake; we'd take four-hour shifts. When we left the dock, you never stopped until you come back unless you had some river stops.

Ike Elkins on River Drives

[Dalkena Lumber Company] built a dam on Caribou Creek, that dam had to hold the water back and they'd bring these logs down and put 'em in the creek. Then they would drive 'em on down into Priest River. Most all of the loggin' had to be done in the winter; you couldn't do no logging in

River pigs near the Thorofare at Priest Lake. Men who moved logs over water were called river pigs; they broke up logjams to keep the logs floating downstream.

the summer. They'd go in the fall of the year to build the roads and they'd start decking logs, but then sleighs hauled in the winter.

Those logs is put into the main river or into the creeks where they had dams back of them. They would close these dams, raise the water and flood the logs on out until they eventually went into the main creeks. In the spring of the year,

The Kalispell Creek Logging Railroad operated from 1927 to 1931.

they would go in where the logs would jam up on the rocks and break those jams. Sometimes they'd have to use powder to break the key log. Then they had this boat that was tapered on both ends and you had to get to that boat or get on the logs as the jam was broken, and take your chances. They had regular men that done the drivin' on the little rivers on account of you had to be a good man on logs. It was kind of dangerous.

JACK MONETTE ON RIVER DRIVES

They get the logs and boom timbers and then they haul them to the sawmills with a tug. That's a boat with an engine on it, and that's the way they hauled them. They just open the booms up and let them go. [A log drive is] a bunch of men on the river, and if they [logs] get stuck on the sandbar or if they get stuck on shore, they push them with pike poles to the sawmills. That's the way it's done. It's dangerous work.

I was one of the good drivers, one of the best. There was a big jam to be broke, and there were six logs ready there for me. They wanted me to take all of them and work at the center jam. Well, I was trying to be 15 minutes late because I wanted somebody else to do it. I'd already broke five jams; I figured it was their turn to break at least one. So George Chriscroft said, "See, Jack, we've got your logs ready for you."

And I said, "What about you guys?" I says, "There's a whole bunch of men here. You're suppose to be good river drivers. Why leave it all to me?"

"Well," he said, "if you can't do it, we can."

So I took my ax and peavey and a pike pole and hit the stumps to that center jam; it took me to 6 o'clock at night to break it. It was getting dark. I thought we'd have to stay there all night. It was getting dark and I couldn't see. So here comes a tall Swede. He was a 6-footer, and he waded in the water as far as he could, right up to his shoulders. When I come to him, jumped with my peavey, my pike pole and ax and saved my tools. I walked wringing wet to my place and put on dry clothes; then I had supper and went back to work the next morning.

WILLIAM WARREN ON SUPPLYING THE MILK TO THE CAMPS

This place sold milk for many years; we actually established what you might call the Warren Dairy in 1936. And then after Elaine and I had been married in 1941, we continued it for 12 years, something like that. We had over 100 head of cows and milked 22 cows many a night.

The dairy business was an awful grind, a long feeding season in the wintertime. We had to put up a lot of hay every year. Very confining. If you wanted to take a trip to Spokane, you had to get up pretty early, get everything done, and then get back and milk the cows in the dark.

Mother and Dad and I moved back here in 1936. The way we got started, we bought two cows and couldn't use all the milk. So anybody that wanted to get fresh milk could come and get it, and we went on from there. Just kind of like Topsy, we grew into the dairy business. Mainly, we would supply the store with bottle milk. There were a few people, three or four sickly or invalids around town, and I would take their milk to them each day. And a lot of people came out here to the place and got it by the quart. And, incidentally, it was 10 cents a quart for many years. The cream on top was so thick you could whip that. Then you'd have a quality underneath that cream was probably better than that 2 percent you buy today.

It was the only dairy here. On the west side there was a fellow by the name of Hoffman up near Lamb Creek; he'd had his dairy for a while. Then another fellow up at Bear Creek tried to start a dairy and said he was going to put all of us out of business by delivering milk along the lake from a big boat he had. He didn't last a short season. We eventually got into the logging camp business, which was much easier for us and supplied most areas. We had one or two camps that would come here and get it from us each morning by 10-gallon cans.

I delivered to Squaw Bay warehouse by 5 o'clock in the morning. Most of the camps would drink, I'd say, 10 gallons. We had one camp up on the north fork of the Priest River; the mailman would come by and pick up a 5-gallon can of milk and take it [as he went back to Priest River] to a junction where the road went into the camp. He would put it in a hole in the ground, put a board over it, and the milk would stay cool until one of the logging trucks would come by and take it to camp. The lumberjacks really liked fresh milk; they would rather drink that than anything when they could get it. And when one of the camps started it, of course, they all wanted it. Then we had to increase our production. The CCC camps, we never did get into them with our product. They required pasteurized milk, and we weren't about to get into pasteurization because it was just too expensive for what it was worth.

We had a milk room here; it was always very sanitary and lots of good hot running water. That's where we washed our bottles, washed our hands, the milking machine and all of our utensils. When we first started, you see, we were milking by hand. Then we bought a [milking machine] with a little gasoline engine. Now this was before we had any electricity in this country. When the gasoline engine would break down, I'd have to milk 22 cows by hand.

Finally we had electricity. I had a little cart that I'd bring milk up from the barn, and Elaine's hard work could start then. In the wintertime, I had a little sled and I'd use it for children's skis. I delivered up to the store that way, too. We had bottle labels printed, "Warren Ranches," we called it. Three ranches in all – this place [in Coolin Bay], the old Chase homestead on Chase Lake and our meadow at Soldier Creek.

We put up hay for 100 head of stock, all loose hay; we didn't bale at that time. Hauled a lot of hay from Soldier Creek meadow. We didn't have any equipment, and there was horse-drawn equipment from early days still on the place. So we rented a team in Spokane, brought them out, and used them that first year so we could get our crops in. But we soon found that it was a whole lot better to get a tractor than to deal with the horse.

In the first place, horses will eat three or four ton of hay. In the wintertime, you might as well be feeding a cow than to fool with horses. If you take care of your herd properly, especially in the real cold weather, you don't let them stand around in the snow. We tried to house just about everything; we had to give them a break in the wintertime. It was a pretty good size barn and we had all of our stalls filled up, and open sheds on one side where the other stock could at least get in out of the cold. The cows themselves would heat it pretty well, really. In extreme weather – we had seen 40 below zero here – I'd go down and milk cows, and I wasn't sure I was going to get to the barn. I actually sat on my hands for a few minutes to get the circulation back and warm them up so I could go ahead and milk.

I made cottage cheese and a little butter and, of course, we made ice cream for our own use. We shipped cream to the cheese company in Sandpoint. In the winter months when we couldn't sell all the whole milk, we would separate and ship cream. It was interesting when the Office of Price Administration came into being [during World War II], we asked for an increase in our milk price because in Spokane they were getting 15 cents and we were only getting 10 [cents]. Two men came here in a great big automobile to talk to us about raising our milk prices. I told them the reason we had to have an increase. But they said we couldn't have an increase, so I told them, "The price goes up tomorrow morning 5 cents. You either come back in the morning and I'll sell you the first quart for 5 cents, or I'll sell you a quart right now for 12 cents, and then we'll take it from there." We never heard from them again.

Barn on Warren Ranch housed dairy cows that produced milk for Priest Lake residents.

The reason we finally quit the dairy business, we could see that the business was going to get larger than we wanted to supply. And the big dairies were looking for this business. We didn't feel that we could handle it with the facilities we had and the long feeding season up here. It's very confining because you have to be here for those two milkings, 12 hours apart. Up until that point, it had been a good business. But the [big] dairies could come in and offer ice cream, butter, cottage cheese, cheeses and everything in the trade.

Nell Shipman with her dogs Lady and Tex in front of the Leonard Paul Store, with Leonard Paul's mother, Amalia, in the sleigh.

Moviemaking with Nell Shipman

Nell Shipman is the most glamorous of all those who failed to make a living at Priest Lake. A vaudeville performer from Victoria, British Columbia, Shipman starred in a series of successful silent movies. In 1920, she formed her own production company and scouted Priest Lake as the setting for a series of outdoor adventure films featuring her menagerie of wild animals. She moved her crew and zoo to Forest Lodge in 1922 and the next year moved up lake to Mosquito Bay to a camp she called Lionhead Lodge. Shipman later wrote in her autobiography: "This was my country, the one spot in all God's world where I belonged. Nature and her wild children would act for me ... not as animated puppets but living, breathing images of wilderness, purity at its divine source."

She made four silent movies at Priest Lake: "Grub-Stake" and three that were part of a series, "Little Dramas of Big Places." The bankruptcy of her production company soon followed, precipitated by the bankruptcy of the independ-

Nell feeding the bears at the Lionhead Lodge, 1920s.

Nell barged her entire zoo of 70 animal actors to the north end of Priest Lake. She is shown here with Felix "Doc" Graff, the animal trainer; they are heading for Sam Byars' Forest Lodge Hotel in 1922.

ent film distributors who represented her films. While some residents fondly remembered the special events Nell Shipman hosted, they also felt resentful when she suddenly left Priest Lake, leaving behind many unpaid bills and dozens of un-cared-for animals. Belle Angstadt kept in touch with Ship-

man after she left and in 1925 quoted a letter reprinted in the Priest River Times. *Shipman expressed faith in yet another screenplay set at the lake, but she went on to say, "Bella, I will use your expression and say, 'The devil has been sitting cross-legged for some time on my doorsill, but I don't fear him for I am not a quitter.' "*

At Lionhead Movie Camp in 1923; pictured are Daddy Duffill, Dot Overmyer, director Bert Van Tuyle, Nell Shipman, Bobby Newhard, leading man Ralph Cochner, Barry Shipman and Laddie.

1922 – Nell Shipman moves to Priest Lake, staying at Forest Lodge

1923 – Shipman establishes Lionhead Lodge on Mosquito Bay

1923 – "Grub-Stake" premieres at Priest River's Rex Theatre in the newly opened Beardmore Block

1924 – Daring winter rescue of Shipman's partner Bert Van Tuyle

1925 – Nell Shipman moves to New York, leaving her Priest Lake debts and animals behind

1977 – Shipman Point officially dedicated at Priest Lake State Park

MARJORIE (PAUL) ROBERTS

A lot has been said about Nell Shipman. They say she was very beautiful, but I remember her more fancy than beautiful. She'd wear a lovely Eskimo-style jacket and hood and extra nice clothes for up here. She set up a camp in Mosquito Bay, a small log sleeping cabin and a float house for the mess hall. One summer the cook's small daughter fell in the water and drowned. I think they beached the house after that. There were cages all over and a large pole barn for the horses. There was an oven built in the side of the hill like a Dutch oven. They baked bread for the animals there.

We used to go up there and see the animals sometimes. In winter they came down by dog sled. In summer they had a fancy speedboat.

One fall they went out to get more backing for their pictures, so they said. Daddy Duffill was left to care for the animals. The food ran out for the animals. When it became clear they had skipped, leaving all their backers and creditors, Daddy Duffill let some of the animals go. But the horses couldn't survive; they ate the poles in the barn. When the ice went out, people got together, loaded the crates on the barge and sent the animals to a zoo.

I can remember the day they brought the animals out after Nell Shipman left. To me, it was just a big holiday. We went down to look at all the animals. I remember there was a cage with a wildcat right close to the edge of the fires, and Abe Lee started to walk around 'em. The wildcat jumped at the cage and kept jumping up and down. There were a lot of hard feelings, not only for the money they cheated everyone out of, but also for the way they left the animals to die.

The Coolin waterfront in 1910 as seen from the lake.

Tourism

It is not surprising that the first permanent building on
Priest Lake was the Northern Hotel built by the railroad to
lure tourists to its pristine shores. If the lake's remoteness and
harsh winters made it a difficult place to eke out a living, the
same qualities attracted visitors who were drawn by its beauty
and abundant fish and game. Before the turn of the century,
visitors came to hunt and fish, camping for weeks on beaches
like those at Camp Sherwood near Coolin or on the long sandbar at the mouth of the Thorofare. Some, like Sam Byars and
Bert Winslow, built cabins on their lakefront homesteads to ac-
commodate the growing number of tourists after World War I.
In the 1930s, others like Ike Elkins and Willard Stevens
bought logged land from the timber companies to set up their
establishments. Regardless of their location, resorts at Priest
Lake remained rustic until the 1950s, which heralded the
arrival of electricity, paved roads, powerboats, ice machines
and huckleberry daiquiris.

1890 – Northern Hotel built at Coolin

1904 – Camp Sherwood established on the Handy homestead

1906 – Idaho Inn serves visitors in Coolin

1914 – Sam Byars builds Forest Lodge at the Thorofare

1923 – Paul-Jones Beach opens in Coolin with rental cabins

1924 – Low's Resort opens in Luby Bay with four cabins

1926 – Lone Star Ranch at Granite Creek leased by Wilson Calfee

1931 – Granite Creek Marina begins

1931 – Jim Low moves his resort to the Narrows

1932 – Elkins Resort opens in Reeder Bay

1946 – Hill's Resort opens in Luby Bay

HARRIET (KLEIN) ALLEN ON CAMP SHERWOOD NEAR COOLIN

I think the Handys named it after Sherwood Forest and called it Camp Sherwood because she had a lot of tourist cabins built in there and wanted them in the summer. In the very beginning, I think they were called tourist cabins.

MARJORIE (PAUL) ROBERTS ON FOREST LODGE

The hotel at the head of the lake was run by Grace Byars all summer through November hunting season. There was a nice screened front porch, a lobby with a stone fireplace, and two deer heads that had locked horns and died that way. [It had] a good-size dining room and kitchen; the second floor had rooms and the third floor had rooms for the help. There was a barn, so they had fresh milk and chickens. There was always fish and venison on the menu. I spent several days each summer up there since Madalyn Byars was only a few years older than me.

Across from the hotel was a long sandbar. Several summers Dad sent all of us – Mother, Betty, June and I, and also the girl who helped mother. We always had a girl help in the summer

Paul-Jones Beach, a partnership between Leonard Paul and Stanley Jones, provided a public recreation area for visitors to Coolin.

to camp on the sandbar. We stayed a month, and the supplies came up with Sam every day. We had two sleeping tents and a cook fly tent. Any company who showed up just came and joined us. We had a rowboat we liked to row to the Upper Lake and then float down.

MARGARET (CALFEE) RANDALL ON COOKING FOR TOURISTS

In the summertime, Mother baked bread, cakes and pies and sold to the tourists. And after Nell Shipman left, Dad bought the stove that Nell used to cook biscuits for her animals.

They had chickens and she had butter, milk, eggs, cream and stuff to do the cooking. The only thing she had to buy was her shortening, flour and sugar. In the fall of the year, we'd go to Priest River and they would buy 10 or 12 hundred-pound bags of flour to use over the winter. We had a cabin next door to the homestead house that had an attic; they'd make a shelf and hung [flour sacks] by baling wire to the rafters so the mice wouldn't get it.

Mother had to make all our bread, and she took care of the garden and did all the canning. We had lots of company, just like the people that live at the lake do. But she was busy cooking for everybody and she had no help. We had lots of chickens and stock cows, but we never ate beef. Every year Dad would fatten one calf and take it to town and sell it for veal at the Priest River store to get some cash money. We used cash money to buy meat and a pound cake from the bakery. That was a big treat.

LODGE INTERIOR, ELKIN'S RESORT   PRIEST LAKE IDAHO

Cozy fireplace in the lodge at Elkins Resort.

MARJORIE (PAUL) ROBERTS ON PAUL-JONES BEACH NEAR COOLIN

Dad and Stanley Jones bought the beach and started building cabins in the 1920s. Elmer Berg came down from his place on Beaver Creek and built the first four log cabins, one each winter. He was an expert with the logs. An old Swede, he spoke very broken English. Later, the other frame [cabins] were built, 16 cabins. They were sparsely furnished, no electricity and outside toilets. The beach was great. There was a water slide and a diving raft anchored about a block off shore where the deep water started. There was a tower, two decks high, and a professional springboard.

When the northern lights were showing, Dad would wake up the vacationers to see them. Not all appreciated it, but none forgot it. We'd go down and wake everybody up and say, "Get out of there and see these lights. You're never going to see them again as beautiful." He'd make them come out in the middle of the night and see those northern lights. They'd cuss and carry on, but in later years they'd say, "I always remember you making me get up; they were very beautiful and I never forgot it."

Everybody knew everybody, and a lot of them came back year after year. A lot of them took [the cabins] by the month and they would help out. The rowboat was part of the cabin; if you had a motor, that was all right, too. So all the kids had rowboats and we'd go out and race and such. They were all these "can't sink 'em" [boats].

Dad never closed up [the Leonard Paul Store] until about eight, but then he'd usually go down and see how things were going. Once a week they had a wiener roast, which Dad called the "get acquainted with neighbors" sort of thing. It was a potluck, and we'd notify everybody up and down the cabins. Mother sort of spearheaded them, and he'd furnish the wieners, coffee and the pop – not pop, but lemonade is what they had. And they'd bring whatever they wanted. That was usually once a week to get the new people acquainted, so they would get to know their neighbors.

It ended with an evening sing-along and swim. They had it from 1923, and then World War II came along. They couldn't keep caretakers and couldn't get repairs, so they sold it.

IKE ELKINS ON THE EARLY RESORT IN REEDER BAY

Well, there was two fellows that owned that old resort down there. It was Bud Jarrett and Tom Jarrett. I loaned them some money on the resort, and they didn't take care of it. They was just about having a good time themselves. When the mortgage come due, they told me if I'd tear up the mortgage, they'd turn the thing over to me. There was a resort on the site where Elkins is now. Winslows had about five old cabins and a few old boats. That was all there was there at that time. There was nothing else I could do, so that is when I acquired it, about 1928. But the fishing was good and I liked to fish and stuff, so I figured it would be a good investment.

I started buildin' and improvin' in the fall of 1932. The Humbird Lumber Company owned this draw that had all this timber on Pine Creek. It was beautiful timber. So I went up and talked to Johnny Humbird, and he says, "Ike, we've lost $3 million here in the last three years, and we're going to liquidate everything we've got in this country." He told me he would sell me that timber, and I could just name my own price. And so I got a loan and bought all those cedar logs, and the whole resort is in cedar.

I had these guys that had been working for me in the woods for years, so I built some of those cheaper lumber buildings up the creek there and put the guys in there. They were the first [buildings]. Then I started the lodge and the log cabins later on. I was a logging for the Ione Lumber Company and they tell me: "Now you can put in so many logs. That's all we want. You can go in and you can put 'em in as fast as you want to or as slow as you want to. But when you get this limit in, we want you to stop." Well, I'd go down there in the summer and I'd put the logs and stuff in, then I'd come back up and work all winter on these buildings.

When we started building, I had two big root cellars there. I had to put in enough food to last all winter on account of the road was open only up to Four Corners, down there at Olson's

Mill. And I had to put in canned stuff to last through the winter, and I would go out and get some deer. I had these logs I was building with, and I had tents over 'em to keep 'em dry. So we'd get some deer and lay them alongside these tents, and we'd shake the snow off the tents and cover the deer. Anytime in the winter when we wanted a deer, we'd go there and get it.

Jim Low on right at Luby Bay in 1924, in a dugout canoe with Tom Lacy.

Camp Pawnee in the 1930s, located at the outlet of Priest Lake.

We always opened on the 15th of April; the fishing opened up then. I had a team of horses and had to pull the cars through the mud down to the resort. Then I'd have to pull them back out. They didn't have to fish very long until they had their limit in those days. Was about $1.50 for most of the boats [to rent in 1933]. We had one we called the *Silver Streak*; we usually rented that for about $3. It was a big boat, about 24-foot long. And the motors, they was all small motors in those days, and we rented them from about $2, maybe sometimes $2.25, $2.50 for them. We never had any trouble about losing the boats we rented, or anything like that. And if we rented a boat out in the daytime, we'd never go to bed until the last guy was in; if he hadn't shown up, we'd go hunt for 'em.

[My family] moved up after we got it [the resort] built. My wife, she'd take care of it when I was in the woods loggin'. She done the cooking part of the time, not all the time. We served meals, but all of the cabins was equipped so they could do their own cookin' if they wanted to. Hugh was our boatman; he was handy, could do most anything. He worked there for a long time. Then Mr. Taylor was our head carpenter; he worked there seven years. Mrs. Taylor done the cookin' in her cabin for people. People would go there [to] get cookies and bread.

Jack Rule was a mean one; he worked there about six or seven years. And Dot Overmeyer, when my wife wasn't there, she was general manager. And Dan Klein worked there all the time we was building; he was there six or seven years. And Roxsey, her maiden name was Rock and her first name was Nora; she worked there for several years. She cooked down at Pullman at the college in the winter. Then she'd come up just on vacation for a while, and finally she stayed year-round.

It took a lot of responsibility off of us [when we got electricity] on account all we had was just motors run by gas. Then at night we had a certain hour we turned 'em off. We had kerosene lights in the cabin, but the customers would squawk a lot of times 'cause we'd turn [the generators] off and leave 'em in the dark.

I got the resort built mostly for a fishing resort. I didn't ever figure on the thing turning out how commercial like it is. And the women got it in their hats to remodel the cabins, build new ones and modernize everything. Of course, they were willing to pay for it, but on the other hand, it wasn't what I started out to do.

Jim Low had a little place down there in Luby Bay. Then afterwards, Hill's bought him out. There was a little resort down there [at] Granite Creek. Stevens owned that piece of property; he bought it from the Dalkena Lumber Co.

Fishing off the docks was a popular family outing for visitors and locals alike.

Rudy Fromme arrived in Priest Lake in 1906 and became supervisor of the Priest River Forest Reserve in 1907.

3.

GOVERNMENT AT PRIEST LAKE

Priest River Forest Reserve

In July 1897, *Gifford Pinchot camped at Priest Lake and observed in his diary that but "for the fires this would be an especially beautiful place." The next year the region became part of the National Forest Reserve System, much to the frustration of area homesteaders and timber companies who were eyeing the lake's vast white pine stands. Pinchot was appointed chief forester in 1905 by his good friend Theodore Roosevelt and went on to create the modern U.S. Forest Service with a zealous vision for conservation.*

For the forests around Priest Lake, this meant managing logging and, especially after the devastating fires of 1910, wildfire prevention and suppression. However, the lake's isolated and undeveloped terrain presented logistical challenges to coordinate men and supplies for firefighting. Before radios, the Forest Service provided the area's first phone system, stringing lines on trees around the lake in order to communicate between ranger stations and the lookouts. The Forest Service established most of the trails to connect and service sites around the lake and up into the mountains. Forest Service boats and barges moved men, animals and supplies around the lake. They initiated area road building, including the West Branch Road from Priest River. Much of Priest Lake's infrastructure today owes its origins to the stewardship of the U.S. Forest Service since 1905.

In 1903, Benjamin McConnell was appointed supervisor of the Priest River Forest Reserve. He was the son of Idaho's first governor, William J. McConnell, and brother-in-law to Senator William Borah. In 1906, Chief Forester Gifford Pinchot sent out Rudolph Fromme, who had recently received his master's degree in forestry from Yale. In an oral history with the Forest History Society, Fromme recalled McConnell's welcome as: "Oh, you're one of those technical guys. I don't know of any technical work around here, but maybe you can make up some. You can sleep in there, and when a fire breaks out we'll take you on it. Of course, if you want to study some of the trees around here or something like that, why you could be doing that." Fromme's experiences at Priest Lake illustrate the tensions within and outside the Forest Service at this time under Pinchot as he used his power to impose management and conservation for the nation's forests. In 1906, the only ranger station was at Coolin, located on the hill just south of the Northern Hotel. For the Goliath task of fighting wildfires, the men commanded only rowboats and pack mules.

1891 – Forest Reserve Act

1897 – Gifford Pinchot camps at Priest Lake

1898 – Priest River Forest Reserve created

1903 – Benjamin McConnell appointed supervisor of Priest River Forest Reserve

1905 – Gifford Pinchot appointed chief forester; creates the U.S. Forest Service in the Department of Agriculture

1906 – Yale forestry graduate Rudolph Fromme arrives at Priest Lake

1907 – Rudy Fromme becomes supervisor of the Priest River Forest Reserve

1908 – Priest River Forest Reserve divided and becomes Kaniksu National Forest

1910 – Forest fires burn 3 million acres in northern Idaho

1911 – Priest River Experimental Station established

1933 – Coolin Ranger Station closes

A Forest Service pack train heads to the government buildings near the Northern Hotel.

LEONARD PAUL ON THE FOREST SERVICE IN COOLIN IN 1906

[Gifford] Pinchot was our first forester. Grover Cleveland inaugurated the Forest Service, but Teddy Roosevelt finally stepped in next. Pinchot went to Germany and found out how the Germans protected their forests and kept them coming. They'd pick up every limb, everything, and you weren't allowed to get any wood in the [forests] any higher than you could reach a limb. Well, he came back and laid it before Roosevelt, and he made him the first forester. So that's why we got those rangers. A few years passed and an edict came out that they had to wear uniforms. They had a regular uniform. [Ranger] Cal Huff, I can still hear him: "Goddamn it, you think I'm going to dress up like a cop?" But they came to it.

Then, you see, the Forest Service reserved the land they had here [in Coolin] for the station, and this used to be head-quarters for the whole Kaniksu Forest, which is now split up into three or four different forests. The supervisor and the rangers and the office force all lived here. The first rangers we had were Sam Davis, Gabe McKenzie, Cal Huff and Dave Coolin. Four of them.

There wasn't even outboard motors then; all we had was a boat that had a hole in the front seat to stick a sail in, and if you had a wind you would stick that sail up. So one day we were all there waiting for the mail at the saloon. You see, there was a hotel, then the saloon, which was a two-story log building, and back of that was a horse barn. Well, we were on the porch of this saloon waiting for the mail, and we saw a hell of a fire up lake. So the rangers were all there too and they said: "My gosh, must be an awful fire at the head of the lake someplace. We better go look. Well, we can't go today, there is no wind. We're not going to row up there." The next day they didn't have any wind. About the third day, they had a head wind and they went up. Two or three days later they came back down. Caribou Creek basin was all afire, [and] they had to report it to Washington, D.C.

RUDY FROMME ON HIS FIRST SUMMER AT PRIEST LAKE

Arriving at Priest Lake [in July 1906] via dusty horse drawn stage, I found Ranger Sam Davis at the supervisor's office cabin, a rather large one-room log affair with lean-to kitchen, about one-quarter mile beyond the end of the road and facing the lake. He said they were expecting me, so he had a mulligan simmering on the wood stove. He said Ben [McConnell, supervisor of Priest River Forest Reserve] was trout fishing in a nearby creek, hoping that the outing might furnish some relief from his summer cold in the head. (I shortly learned that the "cold in the head with nervous perspiration" was McConnell's alibi when trying to sober up from a protracted binge.) Sam further remarked that Ben had been worrying about a big smoke, which lake fishermen kept reporting from up the lake as probably in the Upper West Branch of Priest River.

There were, of course, no telephone lines anywhere on the forest, not even to the little burg of Priest River. He thought we might have to hike over that way from the head of the lake to see if Mike Murray was on the job. McConnell came with the coveted mess of trout, and we three soon enjoyed a banquet but not without a preliminary appetizer from Harvey's [saloon]. My duties for the summer, according to Ben, were to assist Sam in patrolling the 18-mile lake by rowboat (equipped with a sail for favorable winds), and to go to such fires as we could reasonably reach. "Some" he said, "will be too high up, especially lightning fires and not burning anything of value." In case we failed to return after four or five days from fires in good timber, he would send in Tony Lemley, who could carry 80 pounds of provisions on his back. There were no horse trails back any appreciable distance from the lakeshore, and most of the shoreline was not conveniently passable, even on foot. Sam and I confined our backpacking to flour, baking powder and salt (for bannocks), dried beans and rice for vegetables, some bacon (in case we failed to shoot pheasant or fool hens) and dried prunes and raisins (usually wormy) for fruit. He shared his sleeping bag with me, and it called for synchronized turning. He first suggested that we strip down and rub our hides with bacon rind for easier entry, but we managed in our union suits held down with long socks.

I had some face-searing experiences on fires that 1906 summer, but the ordeal I recall most vividly was my first rowing "pilgrimage" with Sam Davis. It was only a 15-mile spin, but my head was spinning long before we got there. Sam's rowboat was heavy, as he carried a pole and sail for favorable winds, but we bucked winds all that first day. My oarsman training had been quite limited, when Sam said, "Now you watch the bend of my body and swing your oars in unison with mine." It sounded easy, but oh, the dead and dread monotony of that bend over, lift oars, mile after mile, to say nothing of searing sun and varying winds. Stealing side-glances at the distant shore, it seemed like we were practically standing still. Then I got to wishing that Sam's metronome arms would drop off, or that the lake would suddenly sink, so we could drag the boat through the muddy bottom for a change. About then Sam's back-swinging oars hit my dragging ones, and I got an explosive, "What th' 'ell's the matter: Tired already? We've hardly started."

Besides my field (and lake) duties with Sam, I assisted the head ranger, Dave Coolin, with organizing and supplying temporary fire crews, preparing time slips and vouchers and punching the Oliver [typewriter] for the supervisor. We hated the thing, but it was a sort of new toy to me. During his more sober periods, McConnell would be raving to catch up on reports and letters. I would then hunt and peck and appeal for repeats. After one of those (office sessions), I started sounding him out on the possibility of developing some commercial timber sale business in the fall. Up he jumped and started pacing the floor, "What the 'ell's bitin' you, Fromme! Don't you like it here? I've spent years teaching everybody that this forest reserve is for the distant future, so far as logging is concerned. W'y, there's already private logging right up to the reserve line on the West Branch, but I've told those timber pirates 'nothing doing.' I don't care a damn what Gifford Pinchot says, and if we just keep our traps shut, people around here will believe me, and go to the Pend Oreille or the Bitterroot or some other reserve, which has been foolish enough to let 'em slip in. But if we once let down the bars to those tree butchers, in will surge a flock of inspectors to look down our necks. You don't want that, do you?

"I tell you, we've got it pretty peaceful here now, except for those barnyard savages (pointing out the side window) from the Palouse country in the summer." This was Mc-Connell's term for the farm families from somewhere below Spokane, who made a practice of camping at the lake for several weeks each summer, so the men could troll for lake trout and the women do the cleaning, canning or salting for winter food. They often pitched their tents or set up burlap barricades quite close to our cabin so that the women and kids, in particular, could be handy to the "government cave o' the winds" as McConnell preferred to call our outside rest-room. This was a very insecure-looking, pole-and-shake struc-ture with a skimpy curtain of burlap tacked across the top of the entrance but extending only slightly below the knees of the visitor. It stood alone and highly conspicuous in the clear-ing alongside our cabin. The supervisor seemed to feel that the women crowded the youngsters into this relief center more often than necessary. I made the remark that it was not attractive to the landscape in any case, and asked why it had not been hidden back in the brush. "Huh," he retorted, "do you make a deliberate practice of hiding things that you may want to find in a hurry?" Instead of the customary mail order catalog, McConnell supplied a heavy file binder of the old pressed letters of former forest superintendents of the Interior Department. He explained that the originals were all in Washington and that nobody had any inclination to read them, at least not here in the office.

An aerial view of The Falls Ranger Station.

RUDY FROMME ON CHANGING THE NAME TO KANIKSU NATIONAL FOREST

[District supervisors] expressed mutual desire to give the old forest a fresh start by changing the supervisor's headquarters to a more thriving hamlet, namely Newport. Paul G. then presented my earlier suggestion to him, that a more appropriate name for the forest would be "Kaniksu." This was the original name given to the large lake, as shown on an old mining map in our files. My information was that it was the name applied by the early day Indians to a favored priest who once lived at or frequented this lake. And so, it came to pass August 1, 1907; the move [to Newport], the new name [Kaniksu] and the new supervisor [Fromme].

Dave Coolin and Sam Davis promptly gave me a bad time when I placed them in charge of our first trail construction project. This trail was to go up Granite Creek from the west shore of the lake. The newly recruited crew – and the bosses –

got so hilariously inebriated at the lodge that they tipped over a rowboat and lost tools, time and tempers. I learned of this fiasco from two non-conformists I had sent from Newport, who came back disgusted. Consultation by phone with Chief Inspector Sherman got them both expelled for six months, and I carried the tidings to the lake via Paul Revere gallops. Boy, was I sore!

LEONARD PAUL ON RUDY FROMME

When Fromme first came, the Forest Reserve wasn't very popular with the home guard here. And, of course, when McConnell came everybody liked him. When they sent out a young man [Fromme] from college from the East, they couldn't understand him. All and all, they got up a petition to have Fromme fired. They brought it down to the store and asked if they could lay it down there because people would come and they would get a lot of signers. I said, "Sure, it's a public place." Well, they said, "Will you sign it?" I said, "No, I won't sign it. The young fellow is doing his duty and it's the law, so let it go at that." A day or two [later] Fromme heard about this petition, so he came in and asked to see it, and I said, "It's right there on the cigar case. Help yourself." He didn't say anything. He knew the feeling of the populace as a whole. There isn't much more I can add except that the girl he married sat across from me in the Priest River School. Her name was Ruby Gowanlock.

A Forest Service work crew poses for a group portrait.

Servicing Kaniksu National Forest

From the original ranger station at Coolin, the Forest Service expanded to more than 10 stations throughout the area with headquarters shifting over time. Before World War II, the Beaver Creek Ranger Station, located on the west side of the lake just south of the Thorofare, became pivotal for fire-fighting operations around the lake and serviced the growing number of lookout towers on nearby mountain peaks. Forest Service rangers were rotated through the system, but local men took on the jobs of packers and boatmen who maintained operations each season.

By 1920, the white pine forests of Priest Lake acquired another enemy besides fire. Blister rust, a fungus brought from Europe at the end of the 19th century, spread to the Pacific Northwest after World War I. The fungus slowly killed mature trees and was devastating for second-growth trees. Blister rust fungus needed two hosts to survive, the white pines and currant or gooseberry bushes. A major effort began in the 1920s to control blister rust by eradicating the currant bushes from the Western white pine forest. Every summer, armies of young men arrived and set up blister rust camps around Priest Lake to clear out the underbrush that supported the fungus. It fell to the Beaver Creek Ranger Station to transport and supply many of these crews working in remote locations.

Beaver Creek Ranger Station was located on the west side of Priest Lake near the Thorofare.

1908 – Priest River Forest Reserve divided and becomes Kaniksu National Forest

1910 – Forest fires burn 3 million acres in northern Idaho

1911 – Beaver Creek Ranger Station, Tule Bay established

1913 – Falls Ranger Station becomes district headquarters

1918 – Reeder Creek Ranger Station established

1916 – Kaniksu Forest Ranger Station, combined Beaver Creek into Priest Lake and Priest River Ranger Station

1920 – National Blister Rust office established in Spokane

1927 – Bismark Ranger Station becomes district headquarters

1934 – Hal Spaulding replaces Les Eddy as district ranger

1940 – Beaver Creek Ranger Station consolidated with Priest Lake Ranger District

HARRIET (KLEIN) ALLEN ON THE FOREST SERVICE

I think the most enforcement of anything was done through the Forest Service. The Forest Service covered quite an area down at the south end of the lake; lots of buildings [and] boats because they had to be getting in supplies. It was a logistics problem, you know, to get things up there quick [to] fires. They maintained very good trails all the way around the lake. Pack trains could go around on them. They ran one single wire phone system along the trails. Every so often in the woods – Indian Creek, Soldier Creek, some of those places – you'd come upon a phone, you'd crank [the handle], call your number of rings with what you wanted.

ERNEST GRAMBO ON THE BEAVER CREEK RANGER STATION

I do remember [Beaver Creek Ranger Station] distinctly. There was a cookhouse, which was on a small knoll behind the lakefront, and then the ranger's house. Those two structures were there and, in addition, a small bath house that was constructed that first summer [in 1930], and it had showers, wash basins and so forth to help the boys coming from work to clean up. The ranger station was a framed construction. The office building was also framed. The cook[house] was of log construction. There was not a barn, but there were corrals and then the sheds under which hay was stored, hay and grain.

Numbers [of mules] varied according to the lift load and the time of the season. Ordinarily, there was only one pack team kept there. But, early in the season when everything was moving out, there would occasionally be two pack strings kept there; nine mules plus the saddle horse on which the packer rode. The packer was always there. He never knew when a pack string might be needed. There were times when there were other pack strings en route [to] other locations in the district. The packers were Forest Service employees. All the supplies came up the lake by barge and by boat to Beaver Creek, or some were transferred to smaller boats and taken up through the Thorofare to the Upper Priest Lake or to the Navigation Ranger Station. And, of course, this also meant that, at times, the supplies were taken from Beaver Creek over to Lion Creek or Indian Creek.

There's an old rumor that there was a gem imbedded in the rocks of the fireplace in the ranger station at Beaver Creek. Do you know that tale?

I know that story very well. Barry Lindaman – he came from Colville – and I found ourselves there at Beaver Creek, and the discussion was [that] Les Eddy wanted to add a fireplace to the old ranger dwelling, and he said, "I located some interesting rock down the lake a ways."

So I said, "Why don't we get it?"

"Well," he said, "it's got to be cut loose from the big mound of it."

Barry and I volunteered. So on Saturday and Sunday, along with Les Eddy, we went down, and that's where we learned how to use a sledgehammer and rock driller and cored out the rock. Barry Lindaman and I carried [the rock] to the boat and from the boat up to where it was used in the building of that big fireplace, which stands today even though the building is long gone. And then Les Eddy obtained the help of some skilled men, I think through the WPA [Works Progress Administration] program, to build the fireplace. He was a geologist so he had a sincere interest in rock and had knowledge as to what would make a good, attractive fireplace. He had specifically selected some rocks, which he found in an area up Caribou Creek and maybe back up in Eddy Peak. He carried them down after having pried them loose from rock, which he had found. I tried to locate this at a later date; never was quite able to find the exact spot that he had mentioned. That's the story behind that fireplace.

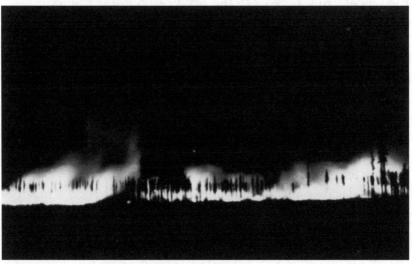

The 1936 fire near Camp No. 159, Company No. 1205.

IKE ELKINS ON FOREST FIRES

The worst fire that ever hit this country was 1910. It jumped the Pend Oreille River, and the Pend Oreille River is a good size river. They were loggin' on the side of the mountain – on the side of the hill there – and the fire run across and started working right where they were loggin'. They had to un-hitch the horses and take them down to a little island in the river to save the horses. Some of those logs burned right on the trucks. They claimed that fire burned as much timber that was logged in the next 25 years.

ERNEST GRAMBO ON FIRE SEASON

We got into our fire season [in 1930] and the district ranger sent me and Ken Nelson to a station up Two-Mouth Creek. At least once a day one of us would go to the top of the ridge and walk for miles looking for fire, carrying a map and a compass, and at nightfall come back down to camp.

[In 1941] we had a new district ranger, Joe Hickman. He landed there just in time to face up to one of the hottest, worst fire seasons that we'd had in many a year. I suppose it was during July that we had one lightning storm that went across the district in the early morning. We received over 100 fires in that one storm. Boy, you turn cartwheels when that happens. Everybody worked, and worked hard.

We had blister rust crews to call on. We also had CCC crews to help us, but it was a matter of walking to fires. [There were] no helicopters and no roads, so it was a lot of walking. I was [fire] dispatcher. I had to figure out how many men we'd need for a certain area, the route of travel, and so forth. In some places, there were six or eight fires in one section. So I sent a crew to a place like that with instructions how to get to all the fires involved. Thanks to favorable weather situations, thanks to a lot of hard work by people who knew how to use tools and weren't afraid of work, we came through that without any major fire.

[Fire dispatching] is a process that is very detailed and must be accurate, and the accuracy starts with the training of the men on the lookout. He has to know how to read maps. He has to know his directions and he has a map before him that has a circle around it. There was a center point on that map board which is the exact location of that lookout. He has an instrument and he circles around a parallel line from the lookout to the spot where he sees the fire. This gives him the location, the section, township and range of the fire location. He writes this down and reports it to the fire dispatcher.

In early days [reporting] was by telephone. At some places

it was done by radio. But at the time I was in that area, it was all by phone. The district fire dispatcher got that information and looked at his map, sees the location, and he had to determine how big a fire [and] what are fuel types there. Sometimes it wasn't very good because we just didn't know that much about the terrain. What timber type it was and other information could help decide how many men must be sent to the fire. The lookout would keep him informed if it is smoking up or firing up.

At nights, sometimes you'd see the fires shoot up and you knew you'd have problems bigger than just one night. But oftentimes, the smoke was detected early. The lookout might have seen the strike come down and would mark that spot and keep his eyes on that, and if fresh smoke started up, why, it was a call into the fire dispatcher and a man was on it. If the fire was real close to the lookout [tower], then the lookout could get there first and take action. When he went to the fire, a man was sent up to take his place at the lookout. Otherwise, if the fire was too distant, help came in from another location, maybe from the ranger station or some other guard station.

We kept no crew at the Beaver Creek station for that purpose. The work crews trained others, like the available telephone maintenance crews. We also had blister rust camps and these were wonderful young fellows, college age, most of them well-trained. They would have practical experience. [They were] a valuable help to us, and in most instances they had been on a telephone line. Later, we had CCC camps, so we could get trained crews to pick up and send to these fires. Each camp was provided with a number of mobile smoke chaser packs. A smoke chaser's pack includes a pulaski, a shovel, and rations, food rations. This was stored in various locations throughout the district.

A pack train of mules is transported across the lake on a barge in the late 1920s.

ERNEST GRAMBO ON BUILDING TRAILS

I was attending high school; I was a senior, 1930, at Mead High School, and I noticed a man talking to the school principal. A little bit later, the man stopped me in the hall and said, "Eddy, would you like a job with the U.S. Forest Service this summer?" Man, I didn't even ask if he was going to pay money. I knew that was something that I would like. We all congregated in early June, the day after the school was out, at Coolin and [took] a boat trip up lake to the Beaver Creek Ranger Station. What it was for a young kid to go up that lake in a boat, headed toward a new adventure; didn't know what it would be, but I just knew, looking at those beautiful mountains and that lovely lake, that it couldn't be anything but good.

First there was a training session to teach us how to use an ax and a saw. The crew that this ranger, Les Eddy, had assembled was mostly from the [Puget] Sound or rural areas. We had a pretty [good] understanding of the work tools that were to be needed and used. Les Eddy was a vet of World War I, had been shot in the jaw and his mouth was twisted over to one side, but you never noticed that. His eyes always sparkled and demanded that you look at him, a nice cheerful sharp smile.

After a training session, I was assigned to a trail building crew. The district was almost without trails when I came there [in 1930]. Building a trail meant clearing the logs, cutting the necessary trees to provide clearance wide enough for a mule to walk along that trail carrying two heavy loads, one on each side. You can imagine carrying a cookstove on one side of the mule [and] weighing down the other with parts of the stove to balance the weight on the mule. The trail had to be wide enough so the mule wouldn't bump into trees.

We started building trails from Two-Mouth Creek up to Grandview Lodge. The trail was located in part by a man known as Jess Underwood. The camp was brought in by mule pack and set up. We stayed in that location, working out of it, up the trail. But as we progressed up the mountain, the walk became longer and longer, and it was necessary to have the pack mules move [the camp] up in the woods, three miles up the trail. We'd return to camp [each day] because that was the cooking outfit, cooking utensils, beds and so forth. As we worked in this camp, we had a pretty good cook, Charlie Brandon. The food and the smell of grub attracted bears. The hams and bacon were hung from the ridgepole of the big fly, which was the place that we ate. There was some food stored in the big tent, a 15-by-16 tent where Al Helm, Charlie Brandon and Harry Miles slept. The young fellows apparently made too much noise for the older men, and we slept in a tent that was 200 to 300 feet away.

Interesting part of the situation was that the bears would smell the food, come to investigate and you can imagine that it caused some disturbance. The cook, Charlie Brandon, told Al

Helm how to take care of the bears: just take a half a stick of dynamite, oh, about six inches of fuse which burned at the rate of a foot a minute, and when you have the bear in the right position, throw this to the side of the road, scaring the heck out of the country. Well, wouldn't you know, it was already dark and Charlie Brandon, who wore a long white shirt and a stocking cap over his nearly bald head, had gone to bed. The rest of us were standing around visiting when we heard a bear through the underbrush very close to the tent 'cause he could smell the hams and bacons out there. [It] had been visiting our garbage dump, no doubt. Al Helm thought this would be a very interesting time to try out the dynamite, I guess. So he had the half stick of dynamite, the fuse, and we stood there in near total darkness but not so dark that you couldn't see something kind of move out there in the brush.

As the bear got closer, Al Helm decided the time was right, so we said, "Now!" I lit the match on the seat of my britches and held it to the fuse, and it started sputtering. Of course, nobody with any sense was going to stand there with a half stick

Watering pack string at Beaver Creek Ranger Station. The Forest Service mules were well-cared for, well-fed and kept in peak physical condition.

of dynamite in his hand and wait a minute or so. He reared back and threw that half stick of dynamite toward the sound of the bear. We held our breath. It hit the small pine tree that had been standing 15 years, 18 feet high. Where did it go? Well, it landed toward the base of the tent. We stood there. I knew that I could run over, pick it up and throw 'em away if I didn't stumble over logs and tent, but we just waited. Finally the big brown tent rose up, but it was tied down securely. Out of the tent ran Charlie Brandon, the cook, in his little white shirt, just screaming at the top of his lungs and followed by Harry Miles, both of them cussing a stream at Al Helm for having been so stupid to do such a thing. We went out to laugh, laugh, laugh. Finally went to bed, and I'm telling the story that stayed with me for the rest of life. Incidentally, Al Helm treated us young fellows very kindly after that. He didn't want the district ranger to find out what he had done.

The following summer when I returned for work at Beaver Creek, the district ranger, Les Eddy, took me out to the end of the dock and said, "See that long rocky road west? I just built the ridge. I want you to take Cecil Stevens and two mules, load up what fresh supplies and official things you want to take, and finish building the trail to the top." We were to go up there, locate the trail and clear the top and build it. Well, I knew how to handle mules since I had experience with horses. [I] loaded up the mules and made my way up to this camp. Set up camp and by nightfall we had enough done so we could at least go to sleep. We tied up the mules and kept them hobbled or tied up with something so they wouldn't run away. Not sure if they would head back to Beaver Creek or not, but we didn't want to chance that.

We start digging on the job. Cecil Stevens, a good ax man, much better than I was, took the ax right into the calf of his leg – a heavy, terrible cut. Well, fortunately, I didn't lose my head. I got first aid supplies – we were well supplied with those – and bound his leg up. Put a compress on it and then loaded him on a big jenny mule and headed back down the trail for Beaver Creek, which was 10 to 11 miles. How fortunate we were that the ax hadn't been across a major artery, but it had been straight up and down; picture it right close to the bone and on the fleshy side

The work crews would put on plays and skits to boost morale. Camp No. 127 foreman Ed Quinn, left, sits with an unknown person behind him and Mr. Frizell. In back are "Tiny" Thompson, Leo Black, Clem Wallace and Peter Hirst.

of the calf on his leg. We arrived at Beaver Creek and, of course, we had no phone. We just walked down the old trail, got to the Thorofare and waded across and into the ranger station. Cecil had the night there, and the next day they took him into Priest River to Dr. Stafford, who was used to seeing an ax cut. Cecil came back in a couple of days but spent the next two or three weeks confined to doing things around the ranger station.

I returned to Beaver Ridge a day or two later. Les Eddy sent up another young man to work with me until we finished building the trail to the top. And then Ken Nelson came to join me, and we were building telephone lines up the mountain. The line would run up Caribou Creek. We had to start from there and build the line up to the top of Gold Peak. Crews brought the wire up to Caribou Creek. It was Ken and I who picked up those 90-pound wheels, carried them around our necks up the mountain. The line was, of course, a grounded line. It was hung on trees. It was a good job that didn't require any skill and was hard work, as we were always walking uphill or downhill and steep terrain.

Pack train headed out of Coolin. The mules were so well-trained they could transport eggs through rugged terrain without breaking them.

Ivan Painter on Building Trails

I started work at Beaver Creek in 1933. There was only two of us hired that year. We built a trail for what they call Trapper Point. We put a tent camp up there. That's a low point just north of Upper Priest Lake so you could see underneath the slope and the smog in the summertime. Then we went from there and finished the trail for Lookout Mountain.

BARNEY STONE ON PACKING FOR THE FOREST SERVICE

At Coolin in 1931, I started packing there. Jim Warden was the ranger for three seasons, and then they shut down the Coolin Ranger Station. The state took it over and sent me down to the Falls Ranger Station. The first year I packed at the Falls for towers and lookout cabins. Then the next year I come [to Priest Lake] in the district lookouts.

Barney Stone brings a pack train to the Squawman Lookout. Some mules carried 160- to 175-pound loads tied on their backs to deliver lumber, supplies and equipment to the lookout.

There was several packers out of the Forest Ranger Station taking care of lookouts and trail crew. I think the earliest [I started] was sometime in April, but generally it was in May. And about the time I got all lookouts and trail camps packed out was generally around the first of October. When I was out packing the towers and cabins, we had our own tent camp. Generally I had a CCC man with me to cook. Working hours were from 4:30 in the morning until 7 or later at night. The mules were owned by the Forest Service; even furnished a riding saddle if you wanted to ride one of them. The lookouts was 10 or 12 miles back; Soldier Creek Lookout was 12 miles. It took all day to make the trip. Get started about 7 o'clock in the morning, might end about 4 or 5 that night. We walked the trails. That was the only way we had for navigation.

IVAN PAINTER ON PACKING FOR THE FOREST SERVICE

There was a CCC spike camp. I had to take the camp down and there was suppose to be someone to help, but there wasn't. So I had to tear that camp down. We got down to the camp; those guys left in such a hurry all the food was left on the table. They was just eating supper. Pots and pans on the stove was full of food, and I had an awful mess to clean up. Some of it I took to the lookout and dumped it off. There was two guys up there building the lookout. I took the lookout's dry camp down and packed it up. It was late in the afternoon when I left there.

Lookout tower at Lookout Mountain with Rex Stuart, 1930.

We got down along the river and it was dark. I couldn't see nothing. I felt something [was] wrong with the pack string, so I stopped with a flashlight and went back. Here was one mule walking around with a packsaddle turned over and the pack down between its legs. What had happened [was] one tent was

Plowboy Lookout located on Plowboy Mountain above the Upper Lake on the west side.

all wet with snow and ice, and I had a little tent with it that was dry. Well, the tent that was all wet with snow and ice had thawed out and got too light and had tipped over. I rearranged everything and put that mule's pack back on again. So it was 8 o'clock before I got back to Navigation, and I dumped all the packs on the beach and put them on the boat the next day. Took care of my mules, give them their supper, went to bed. Next morning, I go to Five-Mile Mountain and packed that off. I packed that right down to Beaver Creek. I did a lot of packing.

IVAN PAINTER ON BUILDING LOOKOUT TOWERS

I'd pack supplies until all the lookouts were supplied. They had eight boxes and one sack, and each of those weighed 160 pounds. The lumber was always transported [to the lookouts]. One year it was all precut. I don't know whether it was put up at Spokane, Missoula or whether they had their shop do it. It was all packaged and the boards were numbered to where they go. The windows and everything was all prepackaged. [The lookouts] had all cement piers under 'em. They had to pack that up, too. We had a spot on the beach near the ranger station that had good sand for making cement. About a fourth of a good sack – that's what they hauled the sand in – and that's about all a person would want to lift. A mule would pack two of them, one on each side. They made the piers right up there.

They had to slide those thin tower poles up there. I remember on Continental Mountain, they had a team of horses rented, one weighed 2,000 pounds, the other one 2,100 pounds. They skidded those trees. I think it must have been an hour and a half. Then they had to build a trail and dig rocks out to make it fairly smooth for those big horses. Horseshoes were about a foot across and they'd catch them there on the rock and tear it off and spend a lot of time tacking new shoes on them. I remember one time I was up there for a couple of days, and I helped a guy that was a teamster. He was a lookout, too, but he was pretty good with horses. He skidded those tall timbers up. In a few places it was so steep you had to put a rock on 'em and walk behind 'em until you got on a place where it wasn't steep. It took quite awhile to put 'em up.

The *Kaniksu* and the *Pend Oreille* were Forest Service work boats.

The *Kaniksu* was a Forest Service work boat used mainly for firefighting on the lake and transporting smoke chasers.

IVAN PAINTER ON FOREST SERVICE BOATS

I went back to the lookout for two years in 1934 and 1935. Then one summer, we covered the big forest fires up in Canada. It got so smoky you couldn't see. You couldn't even see the ground up there. They took me down to Beaver Creek to work around there awhile. Then they had trouble with one boatman and they canned him. They asked me to come into the office one day, and that's when they asked if I could run that boat without too much fooling around. I said, "I'll give it a try." So I started boating then; mostly work was done with the *Firefly*.

The *Kaniksu* was always tied up. That was a fireboat used especially for running down fires on the lake and taking smoke chasers around. It could carry, maybe, 35, something like that. It had a cabin in the back and then a seat in the back, and a roof and deck. There was a front cockpit, and no more than three persons could be up there. We had a 325-horsepower, six-cylinder engine that was put in new in 1935, I believe. The first one wasn't much good because it kept breaking down all the time, so they put a new one in. I think they only paid fifteen hundred dollars for that brand-new engine. I think it took about 30 to 40 gallons to go to Coolin and back. It had two tanks and a spare tank. We had to go to Coolin and back on one tank, some to spare.

It was a boat confiscated by the Coast Guard in Puget Sound. It seems somebody used it for rum running, and they just confiscated it. A year later it was tied up and just rotting away, so the Forest Service got it just for hauling it across the state into Beaver Creek. I think it cost only $500 for the whole trip. It sat on top of the Navigation dock one summer so they could do some rebuilding on it. They had to put some new planks in, fixing dry rot and painted it, and they used it then in 1934, but they didn't have much success with it. It kept breaking down. In 1935, they put a new engine in it and from then on it was a good boat. Every spring I had to work it over, recaulk all seams that needed [it], scrape the paint off. When we got about three coats of paint on, we'd scrape it all down, put new paint on every year and get it ready for the summer.

The *Firefly* was real small. I think it was only 28-foot long and it was pointed at both ends. It would take a couple hours to go to Coolin. Usually, when I towed the barge down that way, it would take about three hours. It was made in Biloxi, Mississippi, or some place around there. It was made out of cypress, and that's a long-lasting wood. It really don't rot, just kind of wears out, I guess. They condemned it and then after it sat up on the beach for a year or so, it was just hard as a rock; just like when it was new. They figured maybe they condemned it too soon.

They had to go through Albeni Falls to get parts, and then they'd route them to Beaver Creek. They sent them to Sandpoint, then Sandpoint would get the part over here. I remember one time I had to get a new propeller shaft, and they had to send

The BRC boat built at Kalispell Bay.

back east for it. The one that was in here was bronze, and the one they got was very heavy and they put on their invoice, "Ship the cheapest way." Well, that propeller shaft took all winter to get here. It came by boat to New York, through the Panama Canal to Seattle, then they shipped it from Seattle to Coolin.

The BRC [boat] was built up there at Kalispell Bay. I'm not sure but that was the *BRC I*. It was kind of an ungainly boat. We all called it a tugboat. It had an old Ford truck motor in it, and that gave 'em nothing but trouble. They condemned that boat and made this boat they called the *Clear Joe*. Captain Markham built that boat right above the boathouse on that flat stretch of ground. He went out and handpicked a tamarack tree, straight grains, no limbs on it, and hauled it down there. Then he had a level spot made with railroad ties, perfectly level, and then he keeled that out of this log. It was the backbone of that boat. When he got through with it, you couldn't tell it was built by hand. It was just as smooth as a marble board. This all done with hand tools, and it took shape there out in the open. That was a blister rust boat used to haul supplies to all the blister rust camps around the lake.

They just condemned the *BRC I* and destroyed it in the

same way as the *Clear Joe* when they got through with it. It was also getting rotten. I don't remember when they got rid of it because I'd left by that time. I left the Forest Service in 1949 and it was still going then. Then the *Kaniksu*, I run that until 1948 and the Forest Service didn't have any use for it, so they loaned it to the state and the state took it over [to] the east side of the lake. They ran it for one year, but they found out they didn't need it real bad. They let it sink a couple of times at the dock, so they nailed it up and put it up in the boathouse, and it sat there several years until somebody from Newport bought it.

That *Pend Oreille* was built in Sandpoint with relief labor. It was built for use on the Pend Oreille Lake and the relief did a pretty good job. They may have done a too good a job. They built a cabin on it, which the boat wasn't designed for. It was just a small launch. I think it must have been about 20 to 22 feet long. The supervisor said, "Get rid of that." The boat wouldn't plane at all. Every time you'd go down the lake [and] if it was the least bit rough, you'd get soaking wet. So the first thing we did was take the cabin off and then we had some carpenter build a winch here for it. Every time I had to change a propeller, I had to pull the boat out of the water. It was a sour job. And finally I got one propeller [that] was fairly good. The boat would pick up a little bit, and we'd make good time with it. I put it in reverse to back up to the dock and, boom, the propeller dropped off. I guess I didn't get the nut tight 'cause it must of spun off. Lost that good propeller, and that was the only one I had like that so I had to try another one. I had to grind it down a little bit and put it in the boat, just about as good as the first one. Then that didn't suit me, so one winter we took it up and put it in the warehouse at Beaver Creek. It was quite a job getting it up there. Just fit in the door. Then I

The *Clear Joe* was built by Captain Markham for the Forest Service.

worked it over; moved the engine back a foot, changed the battery, moved things over in the back. Then it worked fairly good that way. I only run it one year that way, and after that I went in the service.

WILLIAM WHITE ON THE FOREST SERVICE BOAT CLEAR JOE

The *Clear Joe* was a tugboat that the Forest Service used to haul material to the blister rust camps, barge up to the little lake or all around the lake. The *Clear Joe* was 40-feet long and weighed six tons, powered by a gas engine. We had a boat-house at Kalispell Bay. I was the captain of the *Clear Joe*. I'd start operating the boat in May until September. We'd load all the provisions on the tug and we had a 10-ton barge, which we loaded with hay and oats and material. We had as high as 90 men up in the little lake at that time, and there was no roads. They were doing blister rust work, so the only way we had transportation is by boat. We'd take all kinds of food of every description such as meat, potatoes and watermelons, and what have you; hay and oats for the mules. We had sometimes as high as two strings, which consisted of nine mules and two

The *Seneacquoteen* was the official mail boat until 1935.

horses. I hauled the animals back and forth across the little lake many, many times, and out of the big lake through the Thorofare into the little lake. If the water was rough, the mules would sit down, just get down on their haunches and collapse.

IVAN PAINTER ON BOATMAN DUTIES

The *Seneacquoteen* was the official mail boat that went from Coolin to Beaver Creek, and Captain Markham was the one that run that. The mail used to come up there, and they'd come to Beaver Creek and pick their mail up. There was a pigeonhole box in the wall for this person's mail. I think they'd come up three times a week with the mail, and they also had all the freight to deal with. Then people would come clear from Two-Mouth to Beaver [Creek] just to pick up their mail. After about 1935, the Forest Service decided that they could pick up their own mail. I used to go from Beaver Creek down to Coolin three times a week to pick up the mail and get what supplies were needed. All our freight came in there and I'd fill the boat up.

They used to buy some supplies there at Leonard Paul's. But

most of their supplies come from Spokane. And more of their meat, bread and fresh vegetables come from Priest River, and it was delivered up to Coolin, and they'd take it to Beaver Creek. And then later, when they consolidated into districts, everything come in at Bismark, [or] some would come in at Nordman. I took my car over, pick up the mail, get a few supplies – meat, bread and vegetables, stuff like that – and take them back up to Beaver Creek. Then in 1941, we had consolidated into districts and everything was run from Bismark. Then they changed the name from Bismark to Priest Lake Ranger Station.

I came for the mules. They would come in at Cavanaugh Bay. We'd packed 25 tons at a time [on the barge]. I'd bring the barge down there, put 25 ton of hay on it. It would fill the barge up from one end to the other, about four bales high. The Forest Service had two strings there. There's nine mules to a string, with a saddle horse. Then you had extra saddle horses for the ranger to ride. The ranger had a horse, and the alternate had a horse. Then they had a spare horse for the packers. We'd haul them to Mosquito Bay, Squaw Bay and Huckleberry Bay, and go down to Cavanaugh Bay to go to Sundance.

It didn't bother the mules a bit [on the barge]. They'd just stand there and switch their tails. I remember one time I had two strings of mules on when I come from Navigation down to Thorofare towing a barge. I got about to Thorofare and the lake was pretty rough. The wind was blowing pretty hard and when you're pulling a barge, a boat wouldn't turn like a car does. That heavy wake wouldn't let the steering wheel work, so I had to back up and go ahead and turn with the wind. When I backed up, there was a slack in the rope so I could turn a little bit more. I did that about four times so I'd get the boat steered up with the wind and the waves and then come into Beaver Creek. Those guys working there was wondering where the barge was.

All they could see was the mules and a wave of water. And those mules, it didn't seem to bother 'em a bit.

I knew one horse that couldn't swim. One time I was over at Forest Lodge. There's a lot of CCC camps there, and some guy sold beer by the gallon. So this one packer was a small guy; Shorty Lynch was his name. [He] said the packers used to ride their horses around quite a bit. Crossing the Thorofare, they go down near the mouth where it's shallow, and come back up again. Shorty, he was going to swim across. He kicked his [horse] in the sides, and over the bank he went. Pretty soon there was no Shorty, or horse either. So we all make our horses turn around in the water and go back to shore. [Shorty's] horse couldn't swim, wanted to walk on the bottom. That was the only time anybody ever saw a horse that couldn't swim.

One day an old mule took it into his head that he wasn't going to get on that barge. He was the last one, and he wouldn't get on. So the packer unloaded all his mules, then he got on the barge with his saddle horse and started pulling that mule on. That mule would come up to the barge and stand there, just pull and pull and pull. I noticed another packer was getting mad, and I was getting mad and stiff and tired. It wasn't quite dark yet, but finally that mule backed off a little bit. Art give 'em a little nudge and he jumped high enough to jump all over that barge, so all the rest of 'em got back on and we started out.

Then, that night when we got about opposite Elkins and we's kind of dry, so I tied a life preserver on the towline and tipped the boat and let the mules go up the lake. We went over to Elkins and got us a case of beer and come back to the boat, taking that case of beer. In those days it seems like there was an awful lot of beer drinking around the outfit. As long as we kept quiet and didn't raise any fuss, nobody seemed to care.

That was an awful drinking bunch. In 1936, I had 10 pack strings and had to go up to Navigation and then to Beaver Creek. It seemed like every place I stopped with a load of stuff, or stopped to get lunch or something, there's always somebody with a couple of beers to give you. I never did run dry. We really had a good time.

IVAN PAINTER AS BOATMAN AT BEAVER CREEK RANGER STATION

I'd be up there every spring and never get to town until September or October – just stayed up there. They wouldn't let us go. And if you snuck in, you might get down to Coolin the Fourth of July. And that's just about as far as we could go, and we had to go on Colorado time. But we did our celebration on the Fourth of July, and then we had to get back up to the lake on Sunday.

Seems to me at the end of September, or in October, we'd pull a boat up to there. Beaver Creek had a way to pull a boat up, one of those 5-ton hoists. Put it up into the boathouse, then we'd drain all the water out and cleaned it up. Then in the spring, last part of April or May, they'd open Beaver Creek up. Sometimes I'd be by myself; sometimes there'd be a ranger up there. We'd spend a couple of weeks painting and fixing it up for the summer.

Beaver Creek was shut down in the wintertime. The latest I ever stayed up there was December. No boats should have been on the lake about that time. There was a survey crew up there and they got a primary line that was at Upper Priest. They surveyed clear up to East River, almost to Hughes Meadows, and they got through about December, or later part of November. One day they had to go to Granite Creek to do some work and the Bismark [ranger station] was closed. I took them down to the marina and went back to Beaver Creek, and then during the day a storm came up from the north. I went down and picked them up. At Beaver Creek you couldn't tell the lake was rough. When I got down to Granite Creek, the lake was really, really on end. So they were waiting for me. It was about 4 or 5 o'clock; it was almost dark.

Anyway, they loaded in the boat and started out. That lake was on end, and I didn't think I could make it. The spray would freeze the boat in a big hunk of ice. I got partway and thought I'd better turn around and go back. Then I thought, well, if I get in behind Twin Islands it would calm down and I'll make it. I crawled in behind Twin Islands and went around that and got in behind Tripod Point and Discovery Bay, and it was pretty quiet there. Then I couldn't see, so I put her on a compass course and made it to Tripod Point. By the time you got to Tripod Point, you could see Beaver Creek in the dark. There's a sort of silhouette of trees back of Beaver Creek Station. You always aim to get the right spot. When I docked, that boat was a strong mass of ice.

I remember one time I was at the *Firefly* and, oh, it was rough, and I was towing a barge. Then I couldn't make it, so I pulled in behind Eight-Mile [Island] and I happened to have a phone. [On shore] I put the phone up to the telephone line and called into the Beaver Creek, and said I'd be a couple or three hours late until the lake calms down. Late for supper, but I made it.

One time we had a real emergency. There was a guy by the name of Sam Bramer; he was working on trails up the mountain, about 15 miles up in Upper [Priest] Lake, and we got word that he'd put the ax straight in one side of his shinbone. And there was a pack string around there someplace, so they had him go up to Continental Mountain and pick Bramer up. He rode on a packsaddle clear down to the lake.

We figured it would be about 6 or 7 o'clock they'd be down to the lake. They didn't know the circumstances, so they laid a couple of long planks in the back of the boat. After supper, [I] took the boat and went with Grambo's father-in-law – he's a doctor from Denver – and Barney Stone and another packer by the name of Paul Lawrence up to little lake. We got a lot of turbulence on the lake and Ronnie said, "Look at those clouds – they're purple, pink and blue and all different colors." They looked weird. Then all of a sudden, lightning come down on Caribou Hill, and there was one big flash after another. That lake just turned upside down, and the boat would plow under the wave and come into our cabin. We were all three soaking wet, and that doctor was in the back and he couldn't see anything because the waves were so high it was covering the windows and everything. It was all he could do to keep them planks held down so they wouldn't go through a window. That lasted for, I don't know, seemed like forever; I don't imagine it was over 15 minutes, but the boat got full of water. We had to get up to the north end of lake for it to subside a little bit, and we docked the boat. Sam Bramer was hurt pretty bad, but he could walk, and we helped him in the boat. We didn't have to use our plank after all.

I think there was about 90 fires set that night. It seems that everybody was fighting fires. I got just about to Caribou Creek, there was a fire burning and it was burning pretty good, too. So I beached the boat in a gravel bar there. [I] had a piece plank, a fire pumper, all the gas and a thousand feet of hose, and with Barney and Paul, took the hose out. I think they put 200 feet of hose out. I set the pump on the back of the boat, hooked the hose to it and started it up. It seemed like in seven minutes from the time I docked the boat, we had a hold on that fire. Well, we put the fire out and we let the hose lay there because we figured maybe the flames would come up [again]. Ended up at Beaver Creek and, sure enough, there was fire all over the country. I don't remember how Sam Bramer got down the lake. Seems to me that a blister rust boat took him down. Bramer got his leg healed up [and] he came back to work in a short time. Seemed the cut wasn't very deep. And the first aid this doctor gave him on the boat sure helped a lot.

ERNEST GRAMBO ON THE EMERGENCY RUN

During part of this big fire expansion, Helen's [father] was visiting us and brought, as all good doctors do, his medical bag of equipment. He sure had a workout; there were cuts and burns and so forth. He also got a chance to see how things can happen in a big fire. On one occasion, a man had been injured and they took [the doctor] by the *Kaniksu* boat to the head of the Upper Lake to pick up the injured man. He went up there and gave them first aid treatment on the spot. As they were coming down the Thorofare, a fire broke out right alongside of the Thorofare. Ivan Painter, who was the boatman, stopped the boat, hooked up the hose they had for such emergencies, and put out the fire; a wonderful display of good, quick fire action. Ivan Painter took the man to Beaver Creek and he was transported to Coolin, then to Priest River.

CCC camp at Kalispell Bay.

Civilian Conservation Corps Camps

The Civilian Conservation Corps (CCC) proved to be one of Franklin D. Roosevelt's most popular New Deal programs during the Great Depression from 1933 until World War II. The program hired young, unemployed men and sent them around the country for conservation projects on federal and state lands. The CCC, sometimes known as the 3 C's, was organized like the military with a focus on training the young men for future success. The men received $30 a month, but $25 of that was sent to their families back home. At times, there were more than 13 CCC camps between Priest Lake and Priest River. They focused mainly on tree planting, blister rust eradication and trail construction.

1933 – Civilian Conservation Corps created as part of the New Deal

1933 – CCC programs mobilized at Priest Lake

1934 – Luby Bay Ranger Station built as part of the CCC program

1942 – CCC program ended

Annual Yearbook From the Fort George Wright District Civilian Conservation Corp, 1938-39
Kalispell Creek Company History, Co. 281

Company 281, one of the first companies organized at Camp Dix, New Jersey, in 1933, is known as one of the most-traveled companies. Before finding a permanent home at Kalispell Creek Camp, 32 miles north of Priest River, Idaho, Company 281 traveled from coast to coast three times, from Southern California to the snow-capped mountains of Glacier Park, Montana. At Kalispell Creek, Company 281 found a home of which the members are justly proud. Every effort has been made to make the camp a comfortable and pleasant place. Sidewalks were laid out, lawns were planted, a new school building was erected and equipped, the recreation hall was improved, and innumerable other improvements were made. The baseball team pounded its way to the district championship in 1938. Boxing, too, has been an active sport, and two of the district winners were from Company 281. Company dances are given in Priest River each month, and the excellent manner in which they are conducted is a credit to the company.

Due to intensive logging operations in the Priest Lake area, a forest fire destroyed miles of valuable forest. Company 281 was designated to cut the snags, replant and control blister rust in this area. During the year 1938, the members of Company 281, made up of young men from New York and New Jersey, accomplished the following: 575,000 trees planted; 50 acres of white pine seedlings; 8,250 acres of blister rust eradication; 17 forest fires controlled; 90 acres of road right-of-way cleared and burned; 12 miles of roadside snagged; 38 miles of road maintained; 70 miles of trail maintained; 1,100 cords of wood cut; and 2,500 telephone poles cut and treated.

By accomplishing this work, the Priest River area has been changed from a desolate waste of miles of dead snags to a vast garden of vigorous white pine, yellow pine, spruce and cedar. The dividends of this investment, in money value, will not come to this generation. But to the children and the grandchildren of those who did this fine piece of work, it will be a heritage of millions of dollars of good commercial timber, streams well-stocked with trout and game in abundance.

Mona (Elliott) Bishop on the CCC

They had a bunch of boys from New York and New Jersey, and they hauled them up the lake on the barge. They loaded all their stuff on there. It was quite interesting. They had never been out West and they were scared of every- thing. 'Course the locals around told them all kinds

The camps were filled with young, inner-city youths looking for a way to earn a little money.

of stories. That really frightened them. They couldn't, you know, drink water back home, and they'd tell 'em to go get a drink of water, and they wondered where the faucet was, where they could get it. Of course, the wild animals, they were afraid of the bears. Oh, they pulled off all kinds of fun.

William Warren on CCC Camps

[The CCC camps] were all over the area, various spike camps they called them. Spike camps, a small set up, maybe 20 guys, something like that. They would set up and work a certain section of land. They worked on trails and some roads. I really never did see in this particular part of the country any permanent things that they did, except to help the boys get out of the big cities, give them a sense of being and give them something to do. Most of them appreciated it very much. Some of them were renegades and gave nothing but trouble. But they would help fight fire, depending on what the occasion was. It got the boys off the street and out of the cities. In fact, I have known some professional men who stayed in the Spokane area because they came from Eastern states to join the CCC and liked it so well [that] they stayed, were educated here and are in business.

Tent camps housed CCC workers.

ERNEST GRAMBO ON THE CCC

In 1934, apparently the commander of the CCC camp at on the east side of Priest Lake had a couple of characters that were a problem and he wanted to put them out on a trail camp to work on trails or whatever jobs we might have. So I drew the job of heading up this small crew. The approach I took, which worked better than I realized at the time, was to get a good cook. And I had a dandy! They did have problems, but after having a chance to get the good cooking with Bud Owl, it soon became apparent you couldn't drive them away from camp. When we were out locating trails, I knew they would keep on working because the last thing they wanted was to be forced to go back to the main camp. We built a trail up toward Eddy Peak [in 1940]; I became a CCC foreman working for a man named Bill Whetsler. Whetsler headed up planting crews, had a lots of planting done with CCC crews. Quite a wonderful contribution, and how wonderful it was for these young fellows to have a job, to learn how to work and to know they were accomplishing something totally good. A project that I look back at and say this couldn't have been better.

A spike camp at Granite Creek.

Would you explain to me what a spike camp is?

A spike camp is a group, maybe six to 10 men, could have been fewer or more. They set out away from the big main camp; it was a pack with tents and equipment, tools and poles and equipment, and would have been entirely independent from the big main camp and under supervision of somebody like myself.

FULTON MESSMORE ON BUILDING LUBY BAY RANGER STATION UNDER THE CCCs

From 1934 to 1936, I was under the CCCs. You know how that is in the government; you're never sure who you're working for. Everything was supplied by the 3 C's [to build the Luby

Bay Ranger Station]. I boarded there at the camp when my family wasn't with me. There was really no supplies on the job. The 3 C's got the logs, brought them up there and processed them. I got cedar logs and split shingles and shaved them, so everything was done right there on the job. I worked all winter on that cabin. We finished up just in time to come out, and I came down here to start the supervisory office here in Sandpoint in the spring of 1936.

Unidentified men at the Four Corners CCC Camp.

It had electricity but was never plumbed. It was a cabin in all sense of the word. That combination settee and table; they gave me a picture of that. They wanted me to duplicate it. I just wonder whatever happened to this silly thing. Worked all right. All was suppose to be rustic, and it was. Clyde Fiscuss was a government architect at that time. He come up there once. I had no idea where they went to get [the logs]. I know they got one whole set of logs for the building, and they sat there all one winter and blued. By spring, they figured they were no good, threw those all away and went and got some more. Nice white ones. Now they're pretty well blued, too. [The cedar shakes] were all made right there on the job. The

The Four Corners CCC Camp was located between Priest Lake and Priest River.

truckload of CCC boys would clean up every Friday afternoon and haul that all away. It would be two feet deep, all over everything. We had no power tools, of course, and like they did a hundred years ago, go out in the woods and cut trees and build a log house.

I just had those three men and myself for my crew. The rest of them were just extras that would come with another fore-man from the CCC camp, and they just did what I'd tell 'em to do and they'd be gone. Then we'd go ahead with my little crew. They weren't trained. You just had to tell 'em everything. They got pretty adept at it. In fact, one guy went on and worked for me on different jobs later and finally became a contractor here in Sandpoint for several years. We had an older CCC. What do they call 'em? LEMs, Local Experienced Men. They were older people. They found one that was pretty darn handy, and he did the rockwork.

One thing that kind of stuck with me was a bunch of kids come in from the slums of New York, and I could hardly under-stand them, and I guess they couldn't me either because they were always asking me questions. So they were questions, you know, and I'm kind of answering 'em, and after about four or five days of that, one of them sidled up to me, [and] he says: "You know, we're not asking all these questions to find out anything. We just like to hear you talk."

In 1934, I went to work for the government. I worked for the ranger until about the time this Luby Bay thing was finished. Then I got a career job with the Forest Service and went on until I retired. When they hired me and let me go up to Falls Ranger Station, they had a tower for me to build, and it went on from there. Then I got different buildings here and there. Then I built lookout towers for about 15 years. We did lookouts all through the summer. I built a house up there at the old [Bismark] Ranger Station before they moved. I built a five-room house up there, tore down a CCC building to build it.

The Carey homestead at Outlet.

4.

CREATING A COMMUNITY

Housekeeping

Early living accommodations at Priest Lake varied from the dirt-floor hovels of the sourdoughs to several elegant summer homes. The Kalispel Indians pitched their tepees along the sandy shores in the fall, while others without land often took to houseboats that could be moored around the lake. Many of the Swedish and Norwegian immigrants had the best reputation for constructing log cabins, and several like Elmer Berg were sought for their skills. Old cabins were often recycled into new homes, incorporating wood from older structures or moved by boat from one bay to another. Small sawmills like Art Marsten's on Coolin Bay or Fred Schneider's on Kalispell Bay provided milled lumber for many of the lake's homes.

Tepee at Soldier Creek in 1913.

Harriet (Klein) Allen on Building their Cabin

The Chant family had built us a cabin [near Four-Mile Island] because Grandpa [Slee] felt there wasn't a place for Mother to raise us youngsters for summer. Down at Coolin there isn't good swimming right near the marina. And Chant, the homesteader, had come in and built the cabin, expecting to have a homestead of 80 acres. In the first five years it was necessary to prove up on the homestead; they got it done, just about proved up. And then the government created the National Forest system, which included the Kaniksu National Forest, and the homestead rights were canceled. We had the improvements for years because we wanted to farm or whatever, and Grandpa thought that we'd better be close enough to him so we could get back and forth. It would be better for the children to grow up. So Mother had this cabin then. It took them from 1902 to about 1904 to really finish it because they had to cut all the logs and build everything. They had to row from Coolin every day to work. [Later] they had the small *Kaniksu* steamer and was able to tow quite a bit of stuff.

Harriet (Klein) Allen on Early Vacation Homes

It was a Mr. Plummer, who was an attorney in Chicago, [built] a summer home in Indian Creek Bay, kind of in the middle of the bay. I understand he was a partner of Clarence Darrow, representing some of the labor unions and the great labor problems of the Coeur d'Alenes. He brought up beautiful, big, red canoes, and he always had a chauffeur, a handyman and his wife, who was apparently the maid or the cook, to help. They had a good many guests who came. They came on the Great Northern from Chicago, got off in Priest River and came up [to Coolin] and went up [lake] on the steamer.

The cabin was really a very interesting one. It was more

The Handy homestead on Soldier Creek in 1920. It burned in the winter of 1988-89.

like the Great Lakes shore-type summer home or New England shore-type. It had dressing rooms and boat storage and things underneath and several steps up to the porch and the first floor. But that lower part underneath the porch was closed in, lattice work or screen. It was maybe used as a dressing room to go swimming and storing boats and oars and things like that. For years when they weren't using it, somebody had it and lent it to people. The living room and dining room wallpaper was not paper but burlap, green and red, and put on with brass tacks. It had lots of windows and airy space.

HARRIET (KLEIN) ALLEN ON THE BLANCHARDS' HOUSE

The [Ed] Blanchard's large log house [at the Outlet] faced north. I was about 12 and Eleanor 10 when we first used to get together to visit a great deal. It was such fun to do the simple things of those days. Aunt Janie would bake a loaf of orange bread. She would take it from the old woodstove oven, wrap it in a clean tea towel, and put it in a basket with some bottles of

Daddy Duffill's houseboat burned in February 1922, and they lost everything except their fishing poles and the clothes they were wearing.

lemonade, and off we would go in the little old boat with a motor called the *Never Go* for a picnic on some lovely shore. I can see her sitting there slicing a buttered piece off the fresh loaf for each of us.

We all gathered rocks for a big fireplace for one end of the living room. As this was a heavy task, Uncle Ed thought we might as well have a large steel flue up the outside of the house for a chimney and then as we got to it we could cover it with more rocks outside. So he got this big thing like a metal culvert, black, about 22 inches across and about 12 to 15 feet long. He strapped it alongside the old Model T and it stuck out some ahead and behind. They came on the old, twisty mail stage road, and when they got to the beach at the Outlet, they would holler across and someone would row over and get them. Well, it was during World War I and Big Bertha was the name of the largest gun of that war. As Uncle Ed came around one curve in the road, he met another car and the man thought he was being attacked, threw up his hands, ran into the bank and started to run to hide. We loved the fireplace

Pete Chase's trapper cabin, located at the head of the Upper Lake, circa 1912-19.

fires and had one nearly every evening as we sang, played
cards, popped corn or toasted marshmallows.

NELL (CAREY) WHITE ON GROWING UP NEAR THE OUTLET

Living on the homestead, you lived mainly on the land.
Our source of meat was deer and bear and fish. Bears were thick
around here. The soil was just not right for growing gardens;
too much timber and too much acid in the soil. Mom used to go
out and pick ferns in the spring when they first came through
the ground and resembled claws of the chicken. Those big old
coarse bracken fern, when they first pop through the ground,
they're very similar to asparagus. There were dandelion greens
and huckleberries, of course, wild strawberries.

When I was maybe 3 years old, there was a cougar that
came right down back of the cabin. We had a big Airedale dog,
and I was out in the yard playing. I saw this animal and
decided I was going to pet it. So I started for it, and the dog
grabbed me by the back of the dress and dragged me back to

the cabin.

Somewhere my father got a cow. There was no road at that time, but he got a cow so we could have milk. And I can remember one time my mother was out milking the cow and my father was gone. I was maybe three years old and my sister less than a year. So while she was out there, I decided to play in the heating stove with a stick of wood. I got the stick of wood afire and brushed it accidentally against the curtain and up it went in flames, and my baby sister lying in there. Mom looked out through the barn door, saw the flames and came galloping in with the bucket of milk and put the fire out with the bucket of milk. She spanked me soundly after she got the fire out.

My dad used to have a trapline up here and set a trap out on the point as you go across to Coolin from the Outlet. One day we were going across in the boat and he was rowing. He stopped to check the trapline, and he had a skunk in it. So he cracked it over the head, thought it was dead, put it in the boat and we set off for Coolin, and the skunk came to. That's one thing I'll never forget. We finally ended up sticking it in the lake and dragging it behind the boat and drowning it.

I can remember the whitefish running in the mouth of the river and the Indians coming over the hill from the reservation at Usk. They were camping on our beach, and they'd scoop up these whitefish for days at a time, dry them and take them back to the reservation.

MARJORIE (PAUL) ROBERTS ON HOUSEBOATS

Bert Winslow helped Grandpa Slee. There was a houseboat out at the end of the dock that the Winslows lived in. Lots of people lived in houseboats when I was a kid. They just made a floating house; they didn't own any property. They didn't want to buy property, but they could build a house on a float and live there. They'd dock it wherever they wanted to. They could take it up lake and dock it, like the Winslows did. They finally took theirs up to Reeder Bay. They had some property at Reeder Bay, what is now Elkins place, and they would take the house right up there with them. They'd come down here for the kids to go to school. Daddy Duffill lived in a houseboat just inside the Thorofare. He trapped a little and fished, also helping around the hotel run by Grace Byars.

WILLIAM WARREN ON HOUSEBOATS

They were built on logs, big float logs, cedar logs; in fact, when Elaine and I were married in 1941 things were a little tough and we had a chance to rent [a houseboat] for $40 a month. The houseboat was floating in north Coolin. We pulled it down to our property, and Elaine and I lived in that the first winter we were married. It was quite an experience. We even had running water in ours. We saw a spring on the shore and put a garden hose from that spring to our sink and we had constantly running water. We had a chemical toilet in those days. One year later we took it out on to the shore, so when my parents come up, they would have a place.

Why did they disappear?

Well, in the first place it was getting harder to find a place to tie them up. If you owned property, you wouldn't want somebody tying a houseboat to your lot. I think the sanitation laws probably took effect. The Showboat Tavern was originally a houseboat and was pulled up on the shore, and then gradually worked over until [the way] it is now.

Coolin School with grades one through eight and Mrs. Brackendorf, the teacher.

School at Priest Lake

The Priest Lake Public Library and the Coolin Civic Center were originally built as schoolhouses and today serve as reminders of the area's educational heritage. The lake's first school opened around the turn of the century, a little north of Coolin near Soldier Creek, for the early homesteaders' children. Since children had to walk to school, schoolhouses were also built for the Nordman and Lamb Creek communities. These log cabins served as schools but also became the center of community activities. During the winter of 1916, the Nordman schoolhouse hosted a dance every Saturday night. Teachers at Priest Lake, as everywhere else in the United States, were expected to be single women and were forced to quit when they married. The women often boarded with local families or took a room at the hotel in Coolin.

After students finished the eighth grade, Priest Lake families had to make other arrangements for their children to continue their education. Some children boarded with friends

The original Nordman log schoolhouse, 1917. Thomas Kerr, Albert Kerr, Marshall Pettit, Swan Hager and John Nordman built it in 1911. Rose Meyers is pictured with her students.

in Priest River so they could attend high school, while others like Marjorie Roberts went elsewhere to boarding school.

1905 – First schoolhouse already established north of Coolin near Solider Creek

1906 – Change in the Homestead laws brings more families with children

1909 – Second Coolin School built

1911 – Nordman School established

1916 – Third Coolin School built for $1,520, now the Civic Center

1926 – Nordman School destroyed by fire

1934 – Lamb Creek School built by the Works Project Administration

1961 – Priest Lake Elementary School opens, replacing Coolin, Lamb Creek and Nordman schools

1974 – Lamb Creek School reopens as the Priest Lake Library

LEONARD PAUL ON COOLIN SCHOOLS

The first school was at Camp Sherwood, one of those log

Six kids and horse at the second Nordman School. The 1926 fires burned the first school-house; it was replaced with this white, framed structure.

cabins. Most of the children were over on what is now the Cavanaugh Bay Road. There is the great meadow with the Davises, the Reardons and all those [homesteaders]. They could get to Camp Sherwood easier, and Millie Hinkle, a girl I went to school with, was the first teacher. Millie Hinkle batched up there, but the other teachers boarded at the hotel here with Mrs. Handy. By that time the Idaho Inn was built. Then later, we had the new school built up where the water tank is by Paul-Jones Beach. There was a trail from there back to those places [on Cavanaugh Bay Road]. The kids that were in town could get up there, so that was worth it. The third school is the one we've got now. They sold the one by Paul-Jones Beach to Vernon Moulton, Dad Moulton's son. He took it down and built something with it.

Rose (Chermak) Meyers on Teaching at Nordman

I only went to college one year, that's all you had to do in 1914 and 1915. I had filed three applications for my first year. I was 18; had my 19th birthday that December. I hadn't been away from home and didn't know many people. I was raised on a farm 25 miles up on the Nez Perce Reservation and had been no farther than Lewiston. When I signed my contract, they told me where I could stay for the winter. I boarded with [the Kerrs]. I was like one of the family. I didn't have to cook my own meals or anything. I paid board, $20 a month, and then I had my own room. Mrs. Kerr did my laundry and everything.

I came from Spokane to Priest River on the train [and] from Priest River to Coolin on a stage the first week of September. From Coolin to Reeder Bay you had to travel by boat. There was the pretty lake, and I could look up and see Four-Mile Island, and I asked this man if that was the direction we were going. His name was Johnny Malcolm Walker. He was the one that met me [at Coolin] and rowed us across. It took hours. I can't venture how many hours it took, but it took a long, long time. [Mr. Kerr] met me over where Elkins is now. Some people by the name of Winslow were living there at that time and that's where we landed, and Thomas Kerr was there to take me on to his home.

It was quite a little walk [to the Nordman School]; I imagine a mile, a mile and a half, or something like that. I walked it early every morning. It was a log building and I did the janitor work, too, because I got extra pay for that, $15 per month. So by the time I get my wood in and get the sweeping and cleaning done, why it would be dusk or dark. I'd have to walk home in the dark.

You know, the kids and I got along so well. They thought a lot of me, and we had a really good time. They all worked hard and got good grades. On Friday, we always had a little something. We'd have a ciphering match. You chose up sides and then they go to the blackboard and do problems. And we had a spelling bee, too; chose up sides, they liked that, too. Then if I had a chance to get popcorn or something, we always had a little popcorn afterwards. I had one [student] in eighth grade. They had to take an eighth grade examination before they would pass to high school. My kids had the highest grade in this county.

We had parties, and Mrs. Winslow played the violin. We would have box socials several times. I met my husband here; his dad had homesteaded up here. His mother had passed away the year before, and that was 1915. He was only 18, and he and his pals decided they would come to Nordman, stay with his dad and have fun all winter long and go fishing. That's how I happened to meet him. We didn't get married until 1919, after he came home from the service. He went out the same time that I did; I went on home and he enlisted in Spokane in the Navy and was gone for six months.

MARJORIE (PAUL) ROBERTS ON GOING TO SCHOOL IN COOLIN

We didn't have any frills. 'Course we had reading, history and current events and everything that they have now, except we didn't have any art or music or any of that. We went from 9 to 4 every day. Had an hour off for lunch because everybody went home for lunch. It took an hour just to get down the hill and eat and get back up again. It was very seldom in the middle of the winter that we didn't go home for lunch. I remember one winter we had some children that walked in from the Green place, halfway to Cavanaugh Bay. They had to stay for their lunch, so the teacher had to stay for lunch if the children stayed. That winter, periodically, it was a big treat to take

The Lamb Creek School children with teacher, Alyce Allen. This was the last log school used in Idaho.

your lunch [to school]. Soup would sit on the stove all morning, then we'd have hot soup.

When I was in the fourth grade we had to have six children to hold school. We only had four that year, so I went to Priest River because there wasn't enough to open the school. And then about the first of October, Mrs. Egbert came and she had four children, so that did it. She stayed for three or four years. She taught up here and, in order to get her to come back, Dad gave her a place to stay. In the summer he hired her in the store; she got $90 a month. She had four kids, two sets of twins. So she stayed and then when the little set of twins became high school age, she moved to Sandpoint.

MARGARET (CALFEE) RANDALL ON SCHOOL IN COOLIN

We started first grade in Coolin School and went to school

until 1930 when Vern graduated from the eighth grade. We all walked, all the kids in Coolin or around Coolin. We were not that far from town, but we called them the "town kids." The boys especially used to come down to our house because we had horses. There was always something going on. They used to like to go down to the bottom of the lake and go swimming because they could go without their suits on. Those boys! Mother was always baking bread, and she never minded cutting off the heels off the hot bread and giving everybody heels with butter and sugar. My grandmother used to really get upset with her because she'd do that.

At that time there was no school buses. If you wanted to go on to high school, you had to go to a boarding school. Mother bought a place in Moscow, and we went to Moscow. During the time that we lived here, a lot of the people that worked in the ROTC program at the University of Idaho used to come up here and go hunting with Dad, so we knew people in Moscow. Mother bought a house near the campus so she could board students.

Frosty and Scotty Winslow swimming at Reeder Bay, 1915.

Entertainment at Priest Lake

Like today, summertime at Priest Lake brought family and friends together. Parties and dances around the lake attracted summer people and residents alike. Children swam and boated and looked forward to roasting marshmallows at night. Since travel was more difficult, hosting guests became an important ritual – whether it was sourdough Pete Chase at Upper Priest Lake, Belle Angstadt at the Lone Star Ranch near Bear Creek or Leonard Paul on the front porch of his store.

1914 – Church held at the Idaho Inn pavilion

1916 – Fourth of July celebration at Bert Winslow's dance pavilion on Reeder Creek

1916 – "Hard Times" dance at Lamb Creek School, $1 fine for wearing good clothes

1920 – Christmas night social dance at the Nordman schoolhouse

1921 – First radio concert in Coolin at Moore's restaurant

1926 – Opening for the dance hall above the Leonard Paul Store

Marjorie (Paul) Roberts

Tourist season really didn't start until Decoration Day. Decoration Day was the opening of everything around here. The cabins would be full and the tourists would come, and then Labor Day was the end just like it is now except there wasn't so many people around in between. School started and you went to school. The Indians came in October to go white-fishing, and we'd go up [to Sherwood Bay] and visit them for a few days. We'd just go up the Saturdays and Sundays they were here, visit with 'em, talk to 'em. We had our own box socials and little get-togethers, card parties. So it was just like they do now. It hasn't changed that much.

Leonard Paul

The Forest Service finally figured out Priest Lake and Pend Oreille Lake needed a launch, inboard job, so they bought two boats in Minnesota. One went to Pend Oreille Lake and one came to Priest Lake. It was named the *Firefly*. I think it must

New boats head for Paul-Jones Beach.

have been about 24-foot long. It was a big boat.

Well, this [Thomas] Keating and I played around together when somebody [who] was camped across the lake invited us over in the evening for a beach party. There was a bunch of girls there. Of course, Keating would take this government boat and we'd go over. Walt Slee, his fireman and some of his friends would take the steamer he owned and they'd be there; we'd have a dandy time, beach party, swimming, one thing and another. But in the fall of the year when Keating, who was then the clerk here, was asked to give a written report and invoices for the gasoline that was consumed in this boat, he was up against it. He came down to me and said, "Leonard, I just can't make it come out even, you know all those trips we took was charged up to the government for gasoline."

BATHING AT PRIEST LAKE

Swimmers at Coolin Bay.

"Well," I said, "let's see your report. Here you've got so many miles to this fire up lake someplace and you've only put down 18 miles. Just double that mileage and see how you come out." I guess that is what he did because nothing more was said about it.

The Coolin Ranger Station.

Leonard Paul on the Priest River Forest Supervisor Benjamin McConnell

They stressed [Ben] McConnell's accuracy with his .38 Colt automatic. Well, it is a fact! Whenever he would ride horseback up the lake, there wasn't a mailbox along the line that wasn't shot up. He was always shooting. One afternoon when I went to the post office, which was across the road from the hotel on the hill, the stage wasn't in yet so everybody was in the saloon waiting for the mail to come and the bar was all lined up. McConnell was standing at the end of the bar and, of course, he was buying the drinks. So when I came in he said, "Leonard, have a drink." The only place was at the far end of the bar, so I dallied up there and the bartender slid a bottle of rye and a little chaser of water. The glass, of course, had a heavy glass bottom. I poured my drink and looked down in front of all the fellas to McConnell to the end and said, "Here's luck, men." He pulled out his gun and shot the glass right out of my hand in front of all of these people. Of course, all I held was the heavy glass bottom, but it didn't bother anybody. The bartender gave me another glass, I took my drink and finally we got the mail. And that was the end of that. He was unpredictable, no kidding.

Marjorie (Paul) Roberts on Growing Up

We went fishing and hiking and camping out. We had bicycles. Every kid had a rowboat. Almost everybody went down [to Paul-Jones Beach] to swim because that's where the action was. The beach was nice and the kids could go on the slide; there was no charge and no one would bother them. You could go on the big diving ramp, bigger kids and bigger people that wanted to, and that's where everybody swam. This beach and dock was where all the kids spent their summer afternoons and evenings.

There was a beach party every night at Paul-Jones Beach when I was a kid. There was somebody who would have a beach party. If nobody did, well, the caretaker would start one in front of one of the places and everybody would come down and sing along. We'd end up by going swimming in the dark, then go home and to bed around 10 o'clock. It

The Warren-Burch Store on Coolin Beach in 1910. The Joseph B. Slee storage building is on the left. W.W. Slee is in the wheelchair. This group was assembled for a Fourth of July celebration in front of the beach store.

was a big deal. But it wasn't only us kids; anybody that wanted to just came. And if you brought marshmallows, so much the better – if you didn't it was all right.

WILLIAM WARREN ON SATURDAY NIGHTS AT THE RANGER STATION

An interesting thing was that all the phone lines came into this little ranger station [in Coolin], and they had phone lines to all the lookouts on the area's mountains. Every lookout had phone lines. There was no radio, of course, in those days and those lines ran all up through here, through the woods to these lookout stations. And, especially on a Saturday night, we would go into the ranger station. They would have a speaker up on the wall and tied in all those kids all around, clear up into Canada. And, of course, they were lonesome and they put on a show awhile. One guy had some good jokes he wanted to tell, another would have some poetry to read, another might have a guitar, or somebody would sing or somebody would whistle. It was quite interesting. There was a lot of talent and those poor kids were way out there by themselves, you know, trying to hook into civilization.

MARJORIE (PAUL) ROBERTS ON FOURTH OF JULY CELEBRATIONS

There was a large dance pavilion where the post office stands now [in Coolin]. It was open all around with a corner for the band and seats attached to the walls. The Fourth of July celebrations were great; games, greased-pole climbing at the Forest Service dock, swim races at the marina, pie-eating contests at the store porch, other games, which everyone played, and dancing all night. The years when the blister rust camps were going, our front porch [at the Leonard Paul Store] was loaded every weekend with boys sleeping under the shelter. They didn't have much money and had [come] to Coolin for some fun and a change.

HARRIET (KLEIN) ALLEN ON FOURTH OF JULY CELEBRATIONS

What a Fourth of July celebration in front of the beach store! Leonard [Paul] would get lots of fireworks. There would be a boat race between the launches and steamers and rowers; then a big picture of everyone. I remember Grandpa Slee said after a few cars began to come up carefully on those old roads, "I expect to live to see the day when as many as a hundred cars will come up here on a Fourth of July."

HARRIET (KLEIN) ALLEN ON THE COOLIN DANCE PAVILION

They had a very good pavilion and dance on Saturday nights. I remember an orchestra called Mr. Mustard, made up of either three or five pieces. The sax was the loudest. They'd put in 50 cents a person to go and dance. It was just a big pavilion. The ladies sometimes furnished refreshments. People came by boat.

MARJORIE (PAUL) ROBERTS ON DANCES ABOVE THE LEONARD PAUL STORE

It was a big, big opening. You couldn't park from here clear past the Civic Club [schoolhouse]. Dad hired an orchestra. It came

The Leonard Paul dance hall, located above the store, opened in 1926 and was a center of social activity for early Coolin. Dances were held twice a week, on Wednesdays and Saturdays.

up here and lived all summer, and they gave two dances a week all summer long. But on Wednesday and Saturday nights, you just paid at the door and could dance all you wanted to. On Saturday and Sunday afternoon, they had the jitney dances. The orchestra would go up there and practice, and they had it roped off. You just paid at the gate, put your ticket in, and you could dance for one time and had to get off. And that was while the orchestra would do their practice. The next year I don't know what happened, but it didn't pay then to have an orchestra all the time, so he just hired somebody to come in on Saturday nights for the next several years. Just the minute the law went into effect where you could dance in a beer parlor, they raised the restrictions that you could dance for the price of a beer [so] we quit the dances up in the dance hall. We never had any more because Dad didn't want to run a beer parlor.

After Jim and I came home from Japan after World War II, our children were teenagers then. Later, our daughter Charlotte and husband Hank held dances in the hall two nights a week. We'd get 150 to 200 kids up there every night. They

Dancing and beach parties were part of the summer social life at Coolin.

charged 25 cents and that paid for the jukebox. We ran it for two years until it got out of hand. It wasn't the kids that were coming to dance; it was the kids that were coming to raise cane with the kids that were coming to dance. We finally closed it down because it was becoming a nuisance to other people, not to us.

WILLIAM WARREN ON DANCES AT THE LEONARD PAUL STORE

I remember that well. In fact, in 1934 my brother and I came up from San Diego on vacation and found that the hall [above the Leonard Paul Store] was available. They were look-ing for some music, so we phoned back home to San Diego and had our instruments sent up. My brother played trumpet and I played saxophone. We went to the CCC camp in Cavanaugh Bay and found a boy from New Jersey that played the piano, and we opened up the hall. We had two boys from the blister rust [camp] for bouncers, so they took the tickets and bounced the undesirables down the stairway. Captain Markham would take his boat around the lake and pick up people to come to the dances and then take them back home later. Cap would bring the people around to the dance, and they would keep the store open late, which would create a little business and get things cooking around here.

We had some good dances all that summer until toward Labor Day [when] there was quarantine all through the North-west. I believe it was polio. We didn't know anything about it, but we were blissfully going along and getting bigger crowds every Saturday night. Finally, a local woman asked me if we thought we were doing the right thing and I said, "Why?"

"Well," she said, "don't you know that everything in the area is quarantined?" We didn't know that. She said, "You cer-tainly wouldn't want to continue bringing people in here with the disease." So we shut it down right away. We had a real good summer until the quarantine closed us down. We were never actually closed down, but we thought it was the right thing to do when we learned what was going on. Because we were the only dance for many miles around, it really got a good crowd. We had some real good dances.

In those days [at] resorts like Paul-Jones Beach, fathers would rent by the season. Families would come up and stay. In fact, some would even bring maids to help with the children, and the fathers would stay in Spokane and come up on weekends. There were quite a few people here during the summer.

Plowing snow in Coolin. Idaho Inn, foreground; Ida Handy's house, middle; Ed Elliott's house in the background. The Leonard Paul Store would be on right.

Winter at the Lake

Winter isolated early Priest Lake residents even more. Transportation tended to be arduous, depending on the temperature and snowfall. Buggies and boats gave way to snowshoes, skates, horse-drawn sleds and even dogsleds. Most winter residents stocked up on enough provisions to last the winter, but they could still anticipate an occasional Saturday night social at the local schoolhouses. Before electricity reached the lake, harvesting enough ice to last through the year became an important community event. During the coldest years, ice could be cut from Priest Lake bays, but usually the ice came from the smaller, shallower lakes such as Kerr or Chase.

1914 – Whitefish fisherman frozen in at the head of the lake

1916 – Al Roberts skated with the mail sack from Bear Creek to Coolin (12 miles) in less than three hours.

1920 – Deepest ice on the lakes for years because of extreme cold spell and little snow

1920 – Ban on ice fishing

The Coolin waterfront in the winter of 1917. Pictured are Old Northern Hotel, government buildings and the Warren homestead ranch.

MARJORIE (PAUL) ROBERTS

The main road was plowed for horses and buggies and sleighs. [People around the lake] came to [Coolin] that way, or they walked in snowshoes. When [the snow] was really deep, they just stayed home. When they did come, they'd get a room at the hotel and stay a couple of days. Then they'd go back and that would be it for the winter. They just didn't move around

Dogsledding was a viable form of transportation. Pictured is Nell Shipman with son Barry, who traveled 22 miles by dogsled to school in Coolin.

The government dock in Coolin in the winter.

like they do now. And if it was good skating on the ice, they'd
skate home. I've known people to skate down the lake. I never
was good at it and it never lasted that long for me to get good
at it. We'd have good skating and then all of a sudden, snows
pit it. The only time we had real good skating was when we
were cutting ice and they would flood it, and then it would be
good for a couple of weeks.

MARGARET (CALFEE) RANDALL

We would visit people that lived on lake. The only time I
remember going to Nordman was [to see] the Winslow boys;
their folks had moved back to the homestead on Reeder
Creek. They felt so bad about leaving that Mother told them
we'd come to their school Christmas play. So we went clear
around from Coolin to Nordman for that play. That was a long
trip. Dad put a box on some sled runners; we'd hook up the
team with lots of small sleds behind.

Marjorie (Paul) Roberts on Cutting Ice

They would clear a space [on the lake] as big as this house and keep the snow off of it. And then they'd cut a hole and flood it, so the top of the ice would be nice and not have snow on it. Then they'd keep it that way all the time they were cutting. Every night they would do that so in the morning it was nice and fresh ready to go again, and they'd put the ice in the icehouse.

William Warren on Cutting Ice

I hauled an awful lot of ice from Chase Lake for other people because I had one of the only trucks available in the country. Chase Lake would freeze before Priest Lake would freeze. We'd go out there early, clean off a piece of ice as quick as we could stand on the ice and saw around a big chunk, and it would float up a little higher. And then we'd cut it and haul it to various places around here.

How do you keep cutting ice without ending up in the lake yourself?

You have to float a large enough piece, a good big chunk. Depending on the amount of ice you're going to take out, you might have a good score. Stand around with a saw and keep snow off of that piece of ice. And periodically you go out with your saw again and just rip off where it freezes, and then it would gradually keep coming up and coming up. You might build a foot of ice there where there was only 4 or 5 inches off to the side. We had that board marked for the length of chunk you want; you saw off the chunk and then you float it into shore.

Nell (Carey) White on Cutting Ice

They started preparing for it at Chase Lake. A number of different places would go in together and they'd start preparing

Nell Shipman and film crew battle a harsh Priest Lake winter in 1923.

the ice. Somebody would be designated to go there every time it snowed, scrape the snow off and roll a little water on top to smooth it off. I think they began to cut it, if I remember, when the ice was about 8 inches thick. By the time we'd [be] done cutting, sometimes it would be as high as 24 inches thick. They used regular ice saws. They looked like a big crosscut saw with a handle on one end, and they'd hold it upright and saw straight up and down. The first thing they'd do would be thaw out a trough to get [the] blocks up to shore.

How large would a block be?

About 20 inches wide and maybe, at the beginning, 40 inches long. [As] it got thicker and heavier, it would get progressively shorter, and then they'd load it in trucks and haul it. The whole bunch that went together would all turn out when the thawing came in. Some of them would drive trucks, some would saw, some would stay at their own icehouses to pack it down in the sawdust when it was delivered.

[The icehouse would] go below the level of ground about 20 inches or more and start with a layer of sawdust. And then they'd put a layer of ice cakes in and leave maybe 8 inches around the edge; over that was sawdust and all around the edges, and then just build it up gradually with sawdust between each layer. [It would] last all summer. Everybody knew about what they needed. For instance, the Outlet Resort would take maybe 80 tons. We brought 40 tons to Lamb Creek Inn and Farris Resort, which is now Hill's, would put up 120 tons. The end of the ice cutting they all had what they called the Ice Ball. They'd all get together and have a big dinner and a dance, and everybody would get gloriously drunk. That was the highlight of the winter, the Ice Ball.

Ike Elkins on Cutting Ice

We had no electricity in this country in those days, and all the refrigeration in the summer was ice. Everybody in the country would come and get ice here in the winter. We'd just slide it right out of the lake, right up where it would drop into the trucks, and all the resorts and a lot of the private people would come in here and get ice. If the ice was really thick, we'd cut the blocks smaller. But if the ice was thinner, we'd cut 'em bigger; just what people could handle with ice tongs you could lift and slide around. I had a big icehouse down there, built out of logs and had a lot of sawdust. I put sawdust in the bottom and then I'd bring ice in there, and as I packed it I took to filling the cracks all around so the air wouldn't get to it. I'd fill the outside of it and then I'd fill the top of it, and we could keep it all summer there.

All's Fair in Love

Priest Lake's remoteness meant women were scarce. Leonard Paul recalled that sourdoughs and homesteaders were sometimes forced to rely on mail order brides. But as more families began homesteading, schoolteachers tended to present a steady supply of eligible women for the solitary men of Priest Lake. In 1915, the Priest River Times reported that at Nordman: "All our sourdoughs are putting on extra primps these days. The new schoolmarm will soon arrive." The isolation also resulted in more than an average number of divorces, desertions, and "shacking up"; all of which was met with tacit acceptance.

Vera and Leonard Paul, who married in 1914, are shown here in a 1946 photo.

1907 – Belle Hall (Angstadt) kills companion in Priest River; acquitted a month later

1914 – Leonard Paul marries Vera Moore of Blue Lake

1916 – Prize at Reeder Creek party for the bachelor who bid on the best lunch basket

1919 – Marcella Delting, Coolin schoolteacher, marries A.M. Gorsline

1926 – Belle Angstadt dies

Mary Lemley, originally married to Tony Lemley in a mock wedding ceremony, later became his legal wife.

HARRIET (KLEIN) ALLEN ON TEACHERS MARRYING

They could count on the ranger and the teacher getting married. I remember Mrs. Ward came from New England. She was here a year or two and then married a ranger, and they lived here quite awhile. They had three children. She was an excellent teacher. They used to laugh about Miss Ida who married Carl Coolin. She boarded at the hotel [and] was always so cold all winter, and Mrs. Handy had a big wood heater in the living room. [Someone] said, "I never saw anything like that new schoolmarm. She's always so cold and she's working so hard to get Cool." And another one was Marjorie McCormick. Marjorie came out with the Great Northern man at the station at Priest River. She left after about a year.

LEONARD PAUL

Mrs. Handy got this girl, Mary, to come out. She stayed with Mrs. McKenzie that winter, and she got a job at the hotel here. Well, old Bill Bleedhorn wanted to marry her, and Tony [Lemley] wanted to marry her, and she dangled both of them along. Finally, it's deer season and the gang from Rathdrum always came up to hunt deer and they'd stay at the hotel. Among them was a fella named Billy Cleland. He had a livery barn in Rathdrum. They were putting on a party at the hotel one night; I was there. Finally they said, "Well, let's have a mock marriage. Tony, you and Mary stand up," and they stood up in the kitchen. Billy Cleland married them. 'Course, he wasn't a justice of the peace; it wasn't legal, you know. It was a mock marriage, but after it was all over, by God, we said that is legal. "Billy, you are a justice of a peace, aren't you?"

He said, "Yeah, sure."

Mary flew up in the air; she wasn't going to marry that bum of a Tony. Then, Bill Bleedhorn was going to shoot them. Finally, it all cleared up and we told her the truth, but she married [Tony] after all.

HARRIET (KLEIN) ALLEN ON MARY LEMLEY

Everyone has some good yarn about Mary Lemley, who was a misplaced actress if we ever saw one. She was small and quick and loved tea – she drank lots of it or chewed tea leaves like we do gum. When she first came to Coolin, she seemed to be an orphan girl of about 17, they say, and worked in the saloon as a bar maid, cuspidor emptier and mopper-upper. Tony, a frequenter of the bar, proposed to her one day and she turned him down. Then she got to thinking of all those cuspidors to empty and glasses to wash and thought: "My God, what if he doesn't ask me again? It was the Fourth of July and he had a load on, and I sure took him up on it. Drunk when I married him, and drunk ever since!" But then Tony grew more temperate. He built a nice, sturdy home on the river, just below the Outlet, close to a small creek running into the river and just above the first rapids. It was unpainted but had nice windows overlooking the river in both dining room and parlor. The bedroom overlooked a nice large garden, and from the kitchen you could look up the river to the Outlet.

LEONARD PAUL ON BELLE ANGSTADT

Well, Belle was living with this fella, Williams, in Priest River. A very fine fella, he was always nice and kind to me. He had a dray line down in Priest River, and he also owned a ranch that was just across the railroad bridge. He'd cut the hay there, and he also ran the hotel up here and had the mail contract. The reason they never got married was that Belle was a beautiful woman and was married to a banker in St. Louis. She got a divorce and big alimony if she'd get the hell out of St. Louis. So she came to Priest River, then she shacked up with Williams. After they left the hotel and sold out to Abe Lee and his wife, Williams left her, I guess.

She went back living in Priest River and she had another great big fella, and she finally got tired of him and told him never to come back to the house. He was drunk one night and he went up and couldn't get in, so he said, "I'll kick the door in."

She said, "You do and I'll shoot you." She was on the inside with a gun and he kicked, and she shot and killed him right there on the porch. The papers always said the "notorious Belle Williams," but she got out of it. She went to Seattle and Harry Angstadt came down from Alaska, and damned if he didn't run into her. He'd known her; he had homesteaded this ranch up here, you know, got a patent to it. So they got married and moved up [to Bear Creek]; that was Belle Angstadt after that. When Nell Shipman came, they got to be great friends 'cause Harry had a lot of cattle, so Nell would buy the beef. Then when Nell left, Harry followed Nell to California, and that's the last I ever heard of him.

Adventuresome, self-sufficient, courageous and independent defines the Priest Lake woman.

Law and Sort-of Order

Priest Lake's isolation and the independent nature of the residents made enforcement of laws and regulations erratic. Federal and state officials lacked the element of surprise when they came looking for the notorious bootleggers and poachers. And while some might be quick to spread rumors, they would frequently frustrate strangers asking too many questions about fellow residents. Those invested with local power tended to use it sparingly. The arrest and trials of Tony Lemley offers a window into the conflict between law enforcement and close-knit lake relationships. When former game warden Tony Lemley shot his unpopular neighbor at the Outlet, he immediately rowed across the lake and gave himself up to old friend, Constable Art Marsten. After three contentious trials, Lemley was found innocent – on paper, at least.

1914 – Beardmore Stage to Coolin robbed at gunpoint
1916 – Dr. J.M. Clement, wanted for malpractice in Kansas City, arrested at
Lamb Creek

1916 – Tony Lemley shoots T. Frank Green

1917 – After three trials Tony Lemley found not guilty

1926 – "Sourdough Sam" Roland shoots man at Reeder Creek

WILLIAM WARREN ON HIS FATHER, THE JUSTICE OF THE PEACE

My dad's trapping partner, Tony Lemley, was the game warden, and my dad was justice of the peace. They had to hunt up here to make a living. There was no source of fresh meat. Of course, they ate a lot of fish and they canned a lot of things. They had to live off the land, more or less. So, everybody would get a deer when we needed it. They had to be very cautious about how they got their meat because, being the game warden and the justice of the peace, they didn't want anyone see them do it. You might say they were in name only, because nobody bothered [that] the local people were trying to exist off the land. [They considered it] no crime to go out and get a deer or catch more fish than the law allowed. Meat was never wasted. The fish weren't wasted.

At one time, a bunch of people [were] living off the land up on the big meadows near Nordman. From time to time, the game department would send new game wardens to check on things and stop this poaching. The game warden caught a bunch of those people illegally fishing or killing deer, or something, I don't remember exactly. He brought them to the nearest court, which would be my dad's court as justice of the peace. Dad knew all these people, of course, and they had to row across the lake. So he asked them, in turn, were they guilty at all. "Oh yes," they said, "we're guilty."

Dad said, "I tell you what I'm going to do. I'm going to charge each one of you a dollar and cost. I'm going to suspend the fine and remit the cost."

This game warden jumped up and said, "You can't do that."

Dad said, "I can do that, and I'm doing it." The man jumped up again and made a fuss, and Dad said, "That's in contempt of court and will cost you $25." The game warden jumped up again and Dad said, "This time it will be $50." The game warden didn't have any money with him, so they made him leave his gun. Dad kept his gun in his custody until several weeks later the game department sent money to redeem the gun. That was the type of justice they felt should be meted out to people in this area.

There was another time they had a dispute up in that area. Somebody had objected to an outhouse being too close to their property at Deer Creek. So they sent a $20 bill to my Dad for him to make the trip up there to settle this dispute. When he got there, he was able to talk sense into both parties. He said it really looked dangerous, like there was going to be a killing, or something. Of course he wouldn't take their $20 because that was a lot of money in those days for those poor people.

One fall Indians came to whitefish, as was the custom, and some of the young bucks raided a

Tony Lemley shot another homesteader for trespassing on his property and was acquitted.

few cabins around Hunt Creek. They were brought into his court, and the Indian agents said, "You go ahead and punish those boys because they did it." Dad knew that all he could give them was a very small fine, so he remanded them to the court in Sandpoint. Now this was in the fall, and he knew that the court wouldn't sit until next spring. So they sent the Indians to jail in Sandpoint and they had to feed them all winter. Once in awhile, we would get a communication from the sheriff's department to let them Indians go. Dad said, "No, they're in your hands." They would threaten him on his bond as a justice of the peace if he wouldn't let them go. He said, "I read the book they gave me from cover to cover. I think I'm right." In the spring the Indian tribe was on the docket first thing, so they could kick them out of there. But he did give them an offer – minimum punishment [if] they would never bother the cabins again.

It's stealing spawners, fish out of the creek, which everybody did in those days. It was illegal but, again, wardens could let people get whitefish, and they were wonderful fish too. Whitefish is almost extinct in this lake now. When they decided to put the kokanee fish in this lake, they opened the selling of the fish to the public, made it legal. The kokanee was the game fish that could be caught during the summer. They pretty well cleaned the whitefish out in one year by people taking gunnysacks full of them as they run up the creeks to spawn in the fall. Most of them just go up with nets, especially in the moonlight, and catch [the fish] as you'd see them dart by. Or you'd catch them with snares in the daytime with a little noose around their head and give them a jerk. They were a good eating fish but weren't a game fish like the kokanee. People at Priest River and all over came by droves in the fall to steal those fish. I'd say the game warden was pretty lenient.

William Warren on Tony Lemley

Tony [Lemley] had a homestead on the west side of the lake, and he had problems with a neighbor. This man would come through Tony's place and leave the gate open all the time. Tony had some livestock and so he asked [the man] would he please close the gate. Once in awhile, this man would ignore him and just come out of there and Tony would have to go chase his stock and close the gate. So finally one day Tony was sitting on his own front porch and the man came through, opened the gate and drove on, right up to Tony's house. Tony mentioned that, "I asked you to please close the gate." The man pulled out a .22 pistol and started shooting at Tony. Witnesses from the distance said that they heard the small caliber gun, several shots. And then they heard a shot from a big gun, heard another small caliber gun, and then another shot from a big gun, and that was it. Tony had reached inside the door where he always kept the 30-30 rifle. Tony was a wonderful hunter; I still own the gun that killed this man because it belonged to my dad, and my dad had left it there for Tony to use. He said Tony was having trouble with his rifle. They requested Tony into court; practically broke him. He was finally exonerated, but it ruined him. He had gone through all of this and when we came back in 1936, he rowed across from the west side and told us all that had happened.

Harriet (Klein) Allen on Tony Lemley

There was a road that went through [the Lemleys'] place and thereby hangs the tale of the time Tony shot Mr. Green. If someone went through and didn't close the gates, the deer could come in. After losing all the baby beets and carrots a few times, Tony told Mr. Green, a neighbor who often drove through to get to a large hay barn on the next place, to close the gates or the next time he would shoot him. There were harsh words. But anyway, one day Mr. Green drove there in a boastful way and Tony shot him, but was exonerated by the coroner's jury who found he had shot in self-defense as there were bullet holes in his long-handled underwear that were offered in evidence. My grandfather [Slee] was on the jury and always thought perhaps the underwear had been on the clothesline because the holes went through the legs, but there were no holes in Tony. However, everyone was agreed that he had been exasperated beyond endurance and had warned Mr. G. not to trespass. After that, Tony stuck with his cold tea, and I never saw him have hard liquor anytime.

IKE ELKINS ON THE CLAUSEN BROTHERS

In the fall of the year, back in those days, the whitefish run. The lake was full of whitefish and people would come up, catch 'em and smoke 'em. [The Clausen brothers] rented a boat from Stevens' [Marina] and was going up to the head of the lake to whitefish. They got into a storm and the boat capsized. One of them held on to the boat, and the other was away from the boat a little ways. His brother went over to try to help 'em to get back to the boat, and they both went down.

The sheriff and a bunch of guys come up there and they was dragging in the lake. But this water in Priest Lake when it gets down deep, they stay right there. It's just like being in a refrigerator. And so they come to me and wanted me to see if I could get 'em out, and they offered me so much money to take 'em out. The only way I'd do it [was] if I took out one, I'd want so much for taking him out, and then the next one I'd take 'em out a little cheaper. We had a contract to that effect, and this was three months after they went down.

My son-in-law and I went up there and I built this drag. A

fellow named Elmer Berg knew particulars to where they went down, and he told us about where to look for 'em. We didn't have to drag too long until we got hold of one of them. So when we took 'em out and laid 'em out on the dock there, why, he wasn't bloated up or any lips or ears picked off a little by some of the insects in the water. We got curious to get the other fellow, and we drug in there until the ice drove us out, and we never did get hold of the other fellow. So he's in there yet today.

After many years of supporting the pioneers of Priest Lake, Leonard Paul takes a well-deserved nap in his hammock. He was rarely seen without his trademark cigar.

The End of an Era

As in much of America, World War II transformed Priest Lake. The region's isolation disappeared as modern roads connected the lake to the outside world. Not only did new roads snake along the shoreline, but the Dickensheet finally connected one side of the lake to the other. At the same time, electricity became available to all lake residents. New technology transformed the logging industry, which now requires fewer men and eliminated the need for winter camps. The last log drive down the Priest River took place in 1949, shortly before the Outlet dam was constructed. The improved roads, electricity and America's rising affluence changed Priest Lake's tourist industry. Automobile ownership and the growing middle class allowed new generations to vacation at the lake. They flocked to expanding resorts, developing state and federal campgrounds, and to a growing number of lakeside cabins.

With all the changes at Priest Lake, our pioneer voices give a glimpse of an earlier way of life, one more dependent on human ingenuity and endurance. They provide us with the stories behind the area's place names, such as Lionhead Lodge, Nordman or Chase Lake. They bring alive historical buildings, such as the Coolin Civic Center or the Priest Lake Museum. These pioneer voices attest to an earlier spirit that was shared by all who were drawn to Priest Lake.

Bibliography

Allen, Harriet (Klein). Harriet Klein Allen Collection (MS137), Northwest Museum of Arts & Culture/Eastern Washington State Historical Society, Spokane, Washington.

Allen, Harriet (Klein). Interview by Carol Meppen, September 1983 for Priest Lake Museum. Transcribed by the Bonner County Historical Society, Sandpoint, Idaho. Priest Lake Manuscript, Harriet Klein Allen Collection (MS 137), Northwest Museum of Arts & Culture/Eastern Washington State Historical Society, Spokane, Washington.

Bishop, Russ and Mona (Elliot). Interview by Kris Runberg, August 1983 for the Priest Lake Museum. Transcribed by the Bonner County Historical Society, Sandpoint, Idaho.

Elkins, Ike. Interview by G.G. Fisher, 1 September 1983 for Priest Lake Museum. Transcribed by the Bonner County Historical Society, Sandpoint, Idaho.

Fromme, Rudolph. "My Forest Service Memoirs, 1955." In the collection of Charlotte and Hank Jones, Coolin, Idaho.

Grambo, Ernest. Interview by G.G. Fisher, October 1993 for Priest Lake Museum. Transcribed by the Bonner County Historical Society, Sandpoint, Idaho.

Lambert, Junior. Interview by G.G. Fisher, July 1983 for Priest Lake Museum. Transcribed by the Bonner County Historical Society, Sandpoint, Idaho.

Messmore, Fulton. Interview by Ann Ferguson, 25 July 1989 for Priest Lake Museum. Transcribed by the Bonner County Historical Society, Sandpoint, Idaho.

Meyers, Rose (Chermak). Interview by Marcia Knorr, 10 August 1983 for Priest Lake Museum. Transcribed by the Bonner County Historical Society, Sandpoint, Idaho.

Monette, Jack. Interview by Vicki Harter, 23 August 1983 for Priest Lake Museum. Transcribed by the Bonner County Historical Society, Sandpoint, Idaho.

Painter, Ivan. Interview by Janet Wheeler, 11 September 1983 for Priest Lake Museum. Transcribed by the Bonner County Historical Society, Sandpoint, Idaho.

Paul, Leonard. Interview by Marjorie (Paul) Roberts, 9 December 1963. Transcribed by Charlotte and Hank Jones, 2006. Priest Lake Museum Collection, Idaho.

Randall, Margaret (Calfee). Interview by Marcia Knorr, 9 August 1983. Transcribed by the Bonner County Historical Society, Sandpoint, Idaho.

Roberts, Marjorie (Paul). "Old Store" memoirs, 1989. In the collection of Charlotte and Hank Jones, Coolin, Idaho.

Roberts, Marjorie (Paul). Interview by Kris Runberg, August 1983 for Priest Lake Museum. Transcribed by the Bonner County Historical Society, Sandpoint, Idaho.

Stone, Barney. Interview by Ann Ferguson, 9 August 1989 for

Priest Lake Museum. Transcribed by the Bonner County Historical Society, Sandpoint, Idaho.

Warren, William. Interview by Kris Runberg, 18 August 1983 for Priest Lake Museum. Transcribed by the Bonner County Historical Society, Sandpoint, Idaho.

White, William and Nell (Carey). Interview by G.G. Fisher, 12 September 1983 for Priest Lake Museum. Transcribed by the Bonner County Historical Society, Sandpoint, Idaho.

Photograph Credits

All images are from the collection of the Priest Lake Museum and the Bonner County Historical Society Museum with the following exceptions:

Page 104 – Rudolph Fromme from the Forest History Society, Durham, North Carolina

Pages 95, 166, 184 and back cover – Photos by Frank Palmer. Jerome Peltier Collection. Northwest Museum of Arts & Culture/Eastern Washington State Historical Society, Spokane, Washington.

Editor's Biography

Kris Runberg Smith is associate professor of history at Lindenwood University in St. Charles, Missouri. She received a doctorate in American Studies from Saint Louis University, a Master of Arts in American History from Washington State University and a Bachelor of Arts from the University of Idaho in Museum Science. Her great-grandfather, Howard Gumaer, arrived at Priest Lake in 1897, and her family has gathered regularly at Coolin Bay ever since.

Index

Note: Page numbers followed by p indicate photographs.